DO
GOOD
GET
PAID

NATALIE FÉE

LAURENCE KING PUBLISHING

Contents

HOW YOU CAN DO IT 65

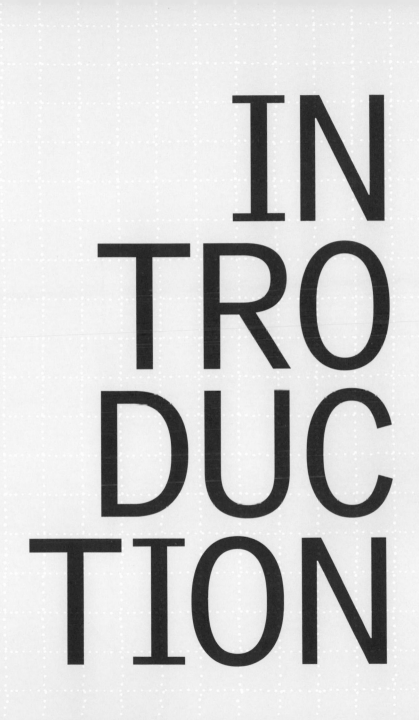

INTRODUCTION

This book is for people who want to make a difference. It's for creatives, campaigners, activists, artivists, craftivists, community organizers, movement builders, changemakers and anyone wanting to earn a living while changing the world for the better. If you've got a campaign that needs funding, or a desire to give up your day job and do something more meaningful, or if you dream of running your own social enterprise, charity or purpose-led business, this book is for you. It's also the story of how I – an unqualified, inexperienced campaigner – ended up starting and running a not-for-profit campaigning organization and making a success of it. I founded City to Sea in 2015; we now have a team of around 20 salaried staff and a turnover of about £1 million ($1.3 million) a year. We're doing good and getting paid … and although we've done our fair share of making it up as we go along, as well as failing and (sometimes) learning from our mistakes, we've also done lots of things right.

These days I'm asked, 'How did you transition from a paid career in television to starting up your own thing?' a *lot*, by all kinds of different people. And that's really what I've set out to answer in this book. As well as sharing anecdotes and learnings from my hotchpotch career path, I'll be sharing the practical steps we took at City to Sea, explaining the magic and methodology we've applied in the hope that you can achieve your mission to *Do Good and Get Paid*. I'll also be sharing stories from other founders, campaigners and creatives to inspire you along the way. From Sabia Wade, the Black Doula, a radical reproductive justice innovator from the USA, to Danny Renton at Seawilding, a project set up to rewild the remote lochs of Scotland, you'll encounter some of the trailblazers I've met, studied or worked with over the past few years, who I'm excited to introduce you to.

The tools and techniques in this book helped me to go from being a single mum on benefits with no savings and little clue about what to do with my life, to setting up a multi-award-winning not-for-profit organization, paying myself and my team and stopping hundreds of tonnes of plastic from getting into our oceans every year, while becoming an author and speaker and raising my son. I acknowledge that, despite being raised by working-class parents, I'm middle class and semi-educated (dropping out of university was a choice; more on that later) and have been afforded many privileges by being a white, able-bodied woman. I hope this sharing of my experience of building an organization, in an accessible way, will go some way to mobilize my own privilege and help anyone who wants to make a difference do just that, while earning a living. So, to all the people who've reached out and asked me how it's done, this is for you. I hope it helps you make a difference to the part of the world within your reach … and get paid doing it!

So, what about you? Amazing, passionate, want-to-make-the-world-a-better-place you! Have you got a burning idea that you want to get off the ground and just need to get this thing funded? Or are you feeling tired and overwhelmed at the scale of environmental and social injustice in the world and can't work out where to focus? Perhaps you're fresh out of college and scoping out your options for becoming a changemaker.

Maybe you already are one. Whatever the case, I hope you'll find some genuinely helpful ideas and inspiration in these pages. We'll be getting into the nuts and bolts of how to build your own thing – whether that's a one-off, kick-ass campaign or a multimillion-dollar operation of planetary healing. And we'll be making sure you've got the right foundations on which to thrive as you go, because burnout is nobody's friend. (We'll also look at what to do if that happens to you.)

We're living through an extraordinary time on Planet Earth

My wish is simply that this book serves as a guide to help you find or create work that's in line with your passion and values and rewards you financially along the way. You're invited to take what you like from it and leave the rest. Dip into it when you need to remind yourself of something, or pass it to a friend who needs some advice. Apply the bits you need, file the parts you don't, and do the next one thing. That's all you ever need to do.

Why the need to 'do good'?

We're living through an extraordinary time on Planet Earth. Gen Z are the first generation to have to face the possibility of the world becoming uninhabitable in their lifetime owing to the climate and ecological emergency. My son's friends talk about choosing not to have kids because, in their words, 'The planet's f***ed, the system's f***ed, we're all f***ed.' We're witnessing a rise of the far right around the world, an unprecedented transfer of wealth and power into the hands of unelected scientific elites (technocracy instead of democracy), and we're still seeing the subjugation of Black, Brown and Indigenous people, and People of Colour, both in 'developed' countries (how developed those of us living in developed countries actually *are* is a not-enough-contested point) and in the majority world. Despite knowing that in order to thrive, we need healthy ecosystems – reciprocal relationships between people and planet – we're still doing a mighty fine job of destroying them. But we're close to something else. Out of the apparent brokenness of our world, green shoots are emerging. Words such as 'regeneration', 'restoration' and 'reparation' are finding their way into the vernacular. Those tender shoots, mostly (and appropriately) arising from grassroots initiatives, are multiplying, connecting and collaborating like underground

Out of the apparent brokenness of our world, green shoots are emerging

mycelium networks, sharing ideas, information and resources. Big companies are doing it too, although inevitably they're conflicted. Still driven by the (perceived) need to increase profits, huge corporations (with the exception of a few CEOs and shareholders with psychopathic tendencies[1]) are populated by human beings who also want to do good. So we're seeing some phenomenally talented Corporate and Social Responsibility (CSR) teams driving incredibly impactful sustainability initiatives. But powerful shareholders and industry lobbyists aren't going away any time soon, so here's to the people on the inside genuinely doing the work to make their company do more good than bad.

Our governments are still dragging their heels when it comes to genuine social and environmental justice, and generally making changes only when there's a financial incentive. Often bribed, lobbied and threatened by big business, most governments around the world are still putting economic progress (which all too often means personal progress for those in power) before a fair and just system that prioritizes people and planet alongside profit. And then there's the seemingly impenetrable, unhealthy relationships between our governments, mass media, big pharma and big business that keep us – the everyday citizens who just want to be able to trust that the world's systems are there to look after us and our planet – locked out of any real decision-making or systemic change.

We have to reverse the destruction of our ecosystems, ideally within the next decade or two, but it won't happen unless we simultaneously address the inequality and injustice that prevent it from happening. Whether your interest lies in building resilient, connected and thriving neighbourhoods, engaging politicians or creating a piece of theatre that transcends divides, now is the time to light a rocket under your arse and make it happen, spectacularly. This book can help, so strike the match and get ready to fly.

What is 'doing good', anyway?

Generally speaking, polarizations aren't helpful. You could be working for an oil company as the person who's banging the drum and pushing for the transition away from fossil fuels and educating your team while secretly microdosing the CEO so that they have an epiphany and stop extractive activities. Is that good or bad? (OK, I went a bit far there, possibly beyond good or bad and into legal/illegal territory.) Or what if you're working for an NGO supporting refugees but the organization won't collaborate with others and is blocking real progress? Good or bad?

My intention in this book isn't to judge anything as better or worse than. Doing good is ultimately a personal, quiet and often private matter. Unless you speak it out loud, no one else knows why you're doing what you're doing (and it's none of their business). You might have a job as a cleaner (as I did about 15 years ago, when my son was little), and through the way you show up, the care you take, the mindfulness you practise, maybe even the eco cleaning products you encourage your clients to switch to, you're doing good by yourself, your employee and the planet. Or you could be working for Amazon in the sustainability department, and by turning one dial to the left a notch you've stopped 600 squillion tonnes of plastic packaging. So don't worry what anyone else thinks: doing good is about doing the right thing by you, your people and your planet. And only you can know if your work in the world is aligned with those three things.

But isn't money the root of all evil?

Money itself isn't a problem, but our relationship with it can be. If we're driven by an insatiable need for more no matter how much we have in the bank, then yes, it's a problem. God knows there are enough billionaires in the world who are still hungry for more. But if we're aiming to have enough – to feed ourselves and our family healthy, fresh food; to pay our taxes; to afford whatever healthcare we need; to travel to where we need to be, when we need to be there; and to live in warm, sustainable homes – then money is simply the means to making it happen. Any more is a bonus (yay!) and can be invested into your mission to do good in the world and to uplift others.

Someone once suggested that my organization was profiteering out of plastic pollution, as though it was a bad thing to pay myself and my team for our campaign work. Go figure. I asked them if they'd be happier if I were making a living working for Coca-Cola, Nestlé or any of the world's top plastic polluters, which actually do profit financially from having their products triple-shrink-wrapped in fossil fuels. At which point they looked suitably uncomfortable and walked off. People may judge you for doing good and getting paid, especially if you're successful. But a) you can ignore them and b) you can challenge the perception that activists and organizers should survive on the goodwill of others and stay under-resourced while they burn themselves to the ground trying to change the world for the better. People who are doing good, and potentially saving countless lives – human, animal and insect – deserve to be well fed, well rested and well rewarded.

People may judge you for doing good and getting paid, especially if you're successful

How much is enough?

Obviously, clarity is needed about how much money *is* enough. Our beloved planet has its limits and we must ensure that whatever we're creating and consuming has a net positive effect on its resources, meaning that the way we operate must be regenerative, not just sustainable.

We can't all live in a mansion with acres of land, travelling around the world to our second, third or fourth homes in our private jets or luxury electric cars. Given that we need to have at least 30 per cent of the planet in its wild state – which includes ensuring the right of Indigenous people to remain in those areas – for it to sustain the biosphere, the planet just hasn't enough space or precious metals for that to happen. Thankfully, not everyone aspires to that lifestyle, but actually, everyone deserves *access* to the luxuries only the super-rich can afford.

... the way we operate must be regenerative, not just sustainable

The environmental journalist George Monbiot calls this notion 'private sufficiency and public luxury'. He writes, 'The expansion of public wealth creates more space for everyone; the expansion of private wealth reduces it, eventually damaging most people's quality of life ... the primary task of all far-sighted politicians should be to decide first how much we can use, then how it can best be shared.'[2] He goes on to explain how decisions should be made by the citizenry so as to effect this – not by the handful of rich individuals who seem to be able to decide what is owned, rented or plundered. So let's see if we can get a sense check on the money part, given this is a book about earning a living doing good.

According to the Office for National Statistics, the national median annual salary in the UK in 2020 was £31,461 ($41,300); in America, calculated by the US Census Bureau, it was $35,977 (£27,412). In the UK, in order to pay rent on a small flat or studio, eat reasonably well and go on one holiday annually, it's generally thought that you need about £2,000 ($2,625) per month after tax (a living wage of around £30,000/$39,375), although that varies massively according to which city you're living in. For a family of four, the figure is around £40,000 ($52,500) for the household.[3]

In the USA, the living wage (as opposed to minimum wage) varies by state. In most states it's estimated that a person or household needs $60,000–70,000 (£45,000–53,000), but California, for example, comes in higher at about $99,000 (£75,500), according to figures for 2020 published by GOBankingRates.[4]

So that's covering the basics. But what do studies say we need to earn in order to be *happy*? Based on a surveyed sample of more than 1.7 million people in 164 countries, research from Purdue University in 2018 found that a yearly income of between $60,000 and $75,000 (£43,600–£56,300) led to 'emotional well-being', whereas a higher annual pay of $95,000 (£74,500) would lead to what the authors of the study called 'life satisfaction'[5]. Interestingly, the study also found that once the magic 'happy threshold' was reached, further increase in income tended to be associated with reduced life satisfaction and well-being.

A study from 2020, by the UK savings service provider Raisin, may give us a more rounded perspective. Analysing data from the Office for National Statistics personal well-being reports and the Happy Planet Index (which tells us how well nations are doing at achieving long, happy, sustainable lives), the study found that the average salary of the top ten happiest countries in the world is over £64,000 ($84,000).[6] But going by the Happy Planet Index alone, Costa Rica comes in at number one; people there live longer and have greater well-being than the residents of many rich nations, including the USA and the UK. All this is achieved with a per capita ecological footprint one-third the size of the USA's. Costa Rica is a success story whereby the government has allocated large amounts of public funding to education, health and pensions, coupled with a strong policy of environmental protection – 99 per cent of its energy is from renewable sources. And what was a typical Costa Rican earning in 2021? About 13,530 Costa Rican colons (£16,000/$22,000).[7] Evidently, where you're born or – if you have the privilege – where you choose to live can make all the difference.

Assuming we can't all move to Costa Rica (we can't; it's not big enough), this should give you an idea of the income you might aspire to for your survival and thrival. But just because the scientists say money can buy you happiness, that doesn't mean you can't be wildly happy living off-grid in the woods. Just make sure you have enough resources to deal with the local rodents. More on that later.

Doing good and getting paid

Let's assume you want to pay yourself enough to live well and help others. As we've seen, there's no golden rule for this, apart from being crystal clear about what you yourself need to earn in order to do your best work. In 'How You Can Do It' (see page 65) I'll take you through the steps you might want to take to get your campaign, project or new business off the ground. But first it might help you to read how I did it. As well as my own founder's journey, I want to share some of my career experiences before I set up City to Sea. This is primarily to give those of you who don't yet know what you want to do, or who are thinking it's too late to switch things up, a sense that you might need to try a load of options before you find your thing. And that sometimes, all those bits of experience you acquire along the way are preparing you for work that's more *you*, even if you don't know it at the time.

I hope my story will inspire you to begin, carry on or start again, and to trust in your power to change the world in whatever way you feel called to. Or just to realize that your career can be a complete shit-show and you still might, eventually, find your way to doing something you love and are good at.

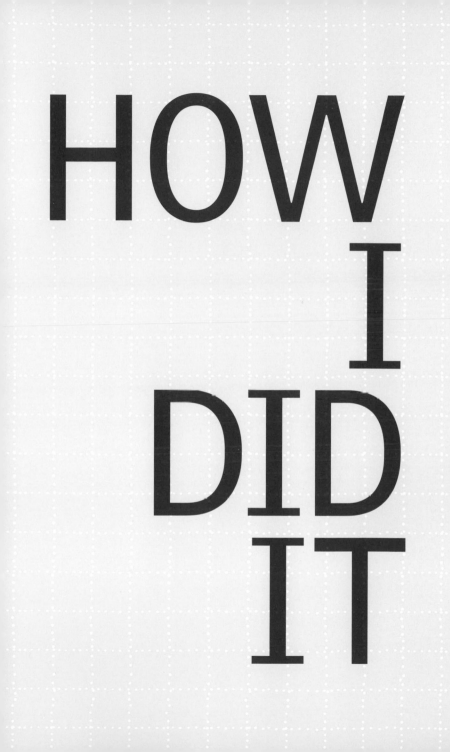

THE HEADHUNTER

3 YEARS

I've often used the term 'coyote trail' to describe my career path. I'll start at the beginning, because people seem to like the fact that an environmental activist began her working life at McDonalds. I won't dwell on it, other than to say that it funded all the things your average 16/17-year-old liked to get up to in the mid-1990s; showed me how incredibly diverse humans are (except when they're drunk, when they all act the same); and taught me how much power there is in a smile, both given and received.

At the tender age of 18 I dropped out of university after just six weeks, feeling uninspired by the course, unsure about what I wanted to do with my life and smoking far too much weed to make sensible decisions about my career. Within a few weeks I had a job as an office temp, getting some admin and 'real-world' experience, as people liked to call it. Mostly I remember wearing new office outfits made of polyester, discovering how cheap, tight-fitting trousers made my crotch smell by the end of the day (important life lesson) and learning to file things … yes, we still had filing cabinets back then. A few months later I went for an interview at an IT recruitment company. I remember borrowing my mum's suit, shoes and necktie and feeling like a total twat when I walked in. Happily, though, I got the job, and began an office career as a junior recruitment consultant.

To say the IT recruitment industry was booming at the end of the 1990s is an understatement – it was exploding. I found out that my natural passion for meeting new people and building relationships with them meant I was quite good at sales. I went from a starting salary of around £16,000 (about $27,000 at the time) as a junior recruitment consultant to earning £60,000 ($90,000) as a headhunter in under three years, thanks to some great managers and the dawn of the internet. It was a fast-track introduction to the world of business, human resources, sales and fat pay cheques. Yet despite the material success, it didn't take long for me to become disillusioned with the lack of meaning and purpose. Was I really on the planet to commute for three hours a day, work for ten, and party or sleep away the rest? If I'd already achieved the things that were supposed to make you happy (a house, a nice car, a good job), why wasn't I happy? Why did I feel empty and unfulfilled? I had a sense that something was gnawing at my conscience, telling me that this life I was living wasn't good for me ... or the planet.

Being young and impulsive, I decided the corporate lifestyle wasn't compatible with my ethical and spiritual yearnings, so, in 2000, aged 22, I quit my job, sold my house, made £15,000 ($23,000) profit, left my boyfriend and bought a ticket to South America, thinking I should plant a few trees and help to save the rainforest. Or find a shaman. Or something. Note to readers: If ever you find yourself earning lots of money at a young age and decide to give it all up to do something more meaningful, *please seek financial advice first. And then act on it.* I mean, no regrets and all, but *why didn't someone tell me not to sell my house?* To be fair, they may have done, but I obviously didn't listen.

SKILLS AND EXPERIENCE ACQUIRED:

✔ Administration

✔ Sales

✔ Networking

✔ Understanding the power of good management

✔ Understanding the power of natural fibres to keep you smelling sweet at the end of the day

✔ CRM (Customer Relationship Management) software

THE ECO VOLUNTEER
1 YEAR

My year spent in Ecuador, Peru and Bolivia was – as I'd hoped – enlightening and transformational. I became fluent in Spanish, learned basic Quechua and spent a lot of time hanging out with and learning from Indigenous families in remote locations from the Amazon to the Andes. I saw at first hand the devastating effects on their communities of mining, extraction and deforestation. I ended up getting tear-gassed in La Paz during the water riots of 2000, and spent time with people and healers who were deeply connected to nature and the cosmos. My reverence for the planet and the people living in harmony with her deepened dramatically, and my former life as a recruitment consultant quickly faded away. I linked up with a local Indigenous activist group and, after living with them for three months towards the end of my stay, decided to come back to the UK and raise funds for them.

My first foray into setting up a charity didn't go well. I was enamoured of a loveable Irish eco idealist whom I'd met in Ecuador, and together we planned a fundraising event in his home town in southwestern Ireland. I decided to spend some of the proceeds from the sale of my house buying local craft products from the communities we wanted to support in Peru and Bolivia, and sell the products in Ireland and at festivals in the UK that summer. I reckoned that 'sleep pillows', small, brightly coloured cushions filled with medicinal herbs, would surely be a bestseller at events. I hadn't considered what UK Customs & Excise would think of my idea. I remember driving five hours to a customs clearance centre to explain what these 500 or so pouches of 'medicinal herbs' from Bolivia really were. Obviously no one believed me, and they had to check it wasn't coca leaves or weed. Anyway, a week later my precious stock was released for me to unleash on the festivalgoers and make sure they all got a great night's sleep.

We called our festival 'DEAF', which, despite being a really bad name for a music festival, we thought was very cool, as it stood for the Dingle Earth Awareness Festival. Not our finest hour. We booked some great bands, people came and paid money, then I gave them *all* food poisoning – performers and punters – by feeding them mussels that volunteers (not chefs) had prepared. It was like a scene out of a comedy movie, with people puking all over the place. I went back to my caravan, projecting liquids from almost every orifice (I was crying by that point too), then

My first foray into setting up a charity didn't go well

miraculously recovered, went back to the festival, jumped on stage and compered the night away to a semi-conscious crowd. I have no idea how we weren't sued. But anyway, we raised about £2,000 for our friends back in Peru, and I left it at that. I didn't think organizing festivals was for me.

SKILLS AND EXPERIENCE ACQUIRED:

✔ Fundraising

✔ Event insurance (for next time)

✔ Importing

✔ Stock-taking (badly)

✔ How not to cook mussels

THE PERMACULTURALIST

1 YEAR

I left Ireland, along with the soon-to-be-ex boyfriend and an unextinguished (despite the copious amounts of rain) resolve to help the planet. Next up: a Permaculture Design Course (PDC) with two of my best friends. I still had some savings left, so I paid for the three of us to do the course. Note to readers: Again, if ever you find yourself with savings, *please seek financial advice before generously blowing them.*

Permaculture ('permanent agriculture') is a way of designing using nature's principles as a model. It's an ecologically sound way of living in households, gardens, communities and businesses – and I found the perfect place to do it. If you've never heard of the Findhorn Foundation, let me fill you in. In the 1970s Peter and Eileen Caddy received guidance from nature spirits telling them to move to this remote peninsula in the northeast of Scotland, next to an army base, and start growing vegetables in the sand dunes. They heeded this, of course (why wouldn't you?), and within a couple of years, with the help of the plant devas (aka nature spirits), they were growing prize-winning, newspaper-headline-worthy giant vegetables. Findhorn is now a thriving example of a world-leading eco-village with nature-based spirituality baked into its ethos.

From Findhorn, PDC certificates tucked under our arms, the three amigas headed south to the bleak but beautiful hills of Hampshire, to put our new skills into practice at the recently established Sustainability Centre in East Meon. Our remit was to build a permaculture garden in return for living in the woods and using the facilities (a converted army base) during the day. Pasci, the most feral of the three of us, was adept at outdoor living, so we put up her bender (a geodesic dome made of hazel, with a canvas cover) next to a clearing in the woods, built a composting toilet and moved in. In October. In England.

We realized we were going to have problems building the permaculture garden on day one, when we found out management wanted it to be built on the old car park. Not on that nice earthy, lawny bit of ground close by, but here, on six feet of concrete. And they wanted a fence around it, which we'd need to erect first. And no, there weren't any power tools. Our naïve enthusiasm for outdoor living and working outdoors waned after a week of trying to dig holes by hand in tarmac and concrete, in the rain. After a couple of months of slow progress and almost killing ourselves from smoke inhalation from our leaky woodburner, we were running out of steam. It was midwinter, the bender was surrounded by snow, and the local rats decided our cosy little shack would be a great place for them to spend winter too. When we heard them scuffling under our beds in dead of night one of us would shout 'RATS!' and we'd all start banging drums (which we kept next to our beds) to scare them off. It wasn't exactly creating the right conditions for restorative sleep. The night I felt a rat *in my hair* was the night I packed my things and went scurrying back to my mum's clean, centrally heated house. We'd lasted six months.

SKILLS AND EXPERIENCE ACQUIRED:

✔ Chopping wood

✔ Carrying water

✔ Lighting a fire

✔ How not to erect a fence

✔ The theory of permaculture (not sure I actually got to put it into practice)

THE YOGINI

4 YEARS(ISH)

At this point I was feeling deflated about my career as a green-living eco-warrior. I'd run out of money, energy and inspiration for living off-grid, and the only constant I'd had that was bringing me joy was yoga. I'd been keeping up my regular moves on the mat for two years and was really getting into it. So, naturally, I thought the next step would be to train as a yoga teacher and share the love – and hopefully make some money, too. A rather special yoga teacher in Southampton, whose classes I'd started attending, agreed to train me. I'd be his yogic guinea pig, upon which he'd learn to be a teacher trainer, and in return, I'd get free training. Boom. Or should I say, Ohhmm?

We worked hard, contorting our bodies, chanting and meditating as though our lives depended on it. I started wearing white clothes, saying 'Namaste' to people and drinking my own urine. Yep, I did say I was really getting into it. Jokes aside, it was pretty cool. I was exploring consciousness, getting fit and strong, and connecting to a community of lovely folk. About a year into my training, my teacher decided to go to India for a year. I was to take over the ashram (actually a Victorian terraced house in a run-down area of Southampton) and run the classes, and the business, while he was away. Off he went, and I stepped up to fulfil my destiny as a yoga teacher and earn a living doing what I loved.

This was it, this was … a positive pregnancy test. I was 24, with a guru-complex and no savings, and I thought having a baby would be a most marvellous thing. (Which, I'll admit, it was.) I reckoned I had about six more months of hardcore teaching in me before I orgasmically delivered my baby on a yoga mat to the sounds of Sanskrit chanting, his first breath a waft of incense. Obviously it was nothing like that, but I did make time to train in pre- and post-natal yoga so that I could carry the yoga spirit with me through motherhood. And running two or three classes a day from the ashram did at least cover my living costs.

I was 24, with a guru-complex and no savings

For the next couple of years, while Elliot was a baby, I just about made a living through my classes, and trained in baby yoga, which was a joy. Seeing the transformation of birth-traumatized babies (and mums) and colicky babies into relaxed bundles of dribble was hugely rewarding.

But after a couple of years, I just felt as though I was done with yoga. Or perhaps I was done with my attitude to it. I was using it as a yardstick, measuring myself and judging myself on how much practice and meditation I was doing, making myself get up at ungodly hours even if I'd had a bad night of breastfeeding half a dozen times. It felt brutal, and I was ready to let it go.

SKILLS AND EXPERIENCE ACQUIRED:

- ✔ Marketing
- ✔ Client/customer care
- ✔ Diary management
- ✔ Bookings
- ✔ Self-employment and book-keeping

THE CLEANER, SPIRITUAL LIFE COACH CUM BUDDING WRITER, AND FESTIVAL MARKETING MANAGER

5 YEARS

My next career move led me to Glastonbury, the UK's spiritual mecca and, according to some, the 'heart chakra' of the Earth. It seemed a sensible move for someone who was dead set on doing work that opened her heart, as well as other people's.

It took a while to get clear on what that was, so I worked as a cleaner to make ends meet. I actually loved it; I enjoyed practising mindfulness and singing along to happy songs as I cleaned, and I liked to think that the care I took in cleaning someone else's house made them feel as sparkly as their surfaces. Slowly, a few more strings were added to my bow – and I diversified my income stream – in the form of writing articles for magazines, doing a radio show, taking people on 'empowerment tours' around the sacred sites of Glastonbury, and a job as marketing manager for a local festival (no, not *the* local festival).

It was the writing part of this 'portfolio career' that was really lighting me up. I'd loved words and books since childhood, but had never thought about writing as a career. My first published article was for the UK-based *Kindred Spirit* magazine, about my experience of the Living with Energy Awareness Training. I was paid about £200 ($350) to write it, and it resulted in around £2,000 ($3,500) of unexpected commission when readers resonated with it and signed up to the training or bought associated products. That was more than I'd earned in a month since my recruitment days, and it felt fantastic.

Buoyed by my first success, I wrote articles for numerous magazines and managed to secure a column, 'The Spiritual Parent', with *Green Parent* magazine. For five happy years I got paid to reflect on and write about the ups and downs of parenting as a single(ish) mum. I also wrote my first book, *The Everyday Alchemist's Happiness Handbook*, which felt an appropriate way to sum up my learning and experiences over the past five years. As a sweet little cherry on top, it was published by Findhorn Press, so I felt as though it would

This was what I'd wanted to 'be' when I grew up, but I'd dismissed it because it wasn't 'spiritual' enough

be beamed out into the world from my second spiritual home. (I'd been back to Findhorn numerous times since my first visit as a wannabe permaculturalist.)

The job as a festival marketing manager gave me more business experience while I built up my writing, tours and, by this point, personal life-coaching service. But wait! There was something else. While travelling and visiting family in Australia when I was 33, I had an experience that stopped me in my tracks. Driving through Sydney, I caught sight of the Australian Film, Television and Radio School. My heart felt as though it was opening, and I started sobbing – a full-body reaction to a sign above a building. Something in me had recognized a long-forgotten yearning to act, perform or be on camera. This was what I'd wanted to 'be' when I grew up, but I'd dismissed it because it wasn't 'spiritual' enough and was all about the ego. But here I was, tears streaming down my face, hearing my heart loud and clear as it shouted out a big, fat YES!

SKILLS AND EXPERIENCE ACQUIRED:

✔ Marketing

✔ Sales

✔ Event production

✔ Sticking to deadlines

✔ Pitching ideas

THE TV PRESENTER

4 YEARS

With a clear sense of what I needed to do next, on returning to the UK some months later I signed up for a four-day crash course in TV presenting in London. 'That should do it,' I thought. And it did, because two weeks after the course I got a gig presenting a seven-hour live YouTube broadcast for a community programme in my home town of Glastonbury. That led to a job presenting the news for GreenTV, which led to work with various online eco content producers. My new career move looked as though it was going to work out. After a year or two building up my experience, I accepted a job as a producer/presenter for an ethical film production company in Bristol.

My time as an all-round right-hand woman to the founder of the production company was perfect. Not only did I get presenting work from time to time, I also got to use my sales and marketing skills while learning about TV production. And, since we were pitching mostly to non-profits and charities, I also met and learned from a lot of interesting people, founders and their causes. At the same time, I was learning to pitch myself and my ideas, as a budding presenter, to other TV companies. That was inevitably pretty soul-destroying since I'd much rather be selling a worthy cause or product than selling myself. But I did it because I had a heap of ideas for programmes that I knew would educate and engage people on well-being and the environment.

In terms of embracing rejection and failure, this period was my most formative. It sucked. 'It's too worthy' or 'people just won't be interested' were the main reasons for the consistent 'no' I was getting. It seemed as though the odds were stacked against me. Until, at last, local TV got a big funding boost in the UK in 2015, and Bristol got its own TV channel. I managed to get a job as a producer/presenter for a daily show, which I named *The Source*, and my wayward, loveable, You-Tubing co-presenter Jack Maynard and I clocked up over 250 hours of prime-time telly.

... in my precious spare time, something more mean-ingful was taking root

But while interviewing some of my favourite celebrities was fun, my motivation for being on TV was to do good, so I persistently tried to steer the content towards the more meaningful social and environmental feel-good stories, of which there were lots to choose from in Bristol. Sadly, that wasn't the directive of the channel, or my show, as it turned out, and management wanted more glitz, glamour and showbiz – generally the stuff that didn't excite me or make me feel I was contributing anything worthwhile to the ecological emergency unfolding around the world. Meanwhile, in my precious spare time, something more meaningful was taking root.

SKILLS AND EXPERIENCE ACQUIRED:

✔ Presenting

✔ Broadcast journalism

✔ TV production: basic sound, lighting, editing etc.

✔ Live TV

✔ Interviewing techniques

✔ Pitching for work

✔ How to deal with failure

THE FOUNDER
7 YEARS (AND COUNTING)

A wake-up call (or squawk)

Moments after watching the trailer for the film *Albatross* by the American artist Chris Jordan in 2014, something shifted in me. Or rather, something broke open. I was at home, scrolling through Facebook, and up popped this video about the plight of the Laysan albatrosses, dying of starvation in their nests, their bellies full of plastic. It was the music that captured my attention, a hauntingly beautiful guitar and pan pipes composition that felt like a spiritual experience in itself. (I ended up meeting the composer, Al Lethbridge, four years later, on finding out that he lived about four doors down from my office in Bristol.)

For three minutes I was transported into Chris's world and experienced the beauty, joy and tragedy unfolding in the nests of these majestic birds in the central Pacific. In the decaying remains of thousands of fluffy chicks, I recognized everyday plastic items that I was using. I recognized the names and logos of the big brands on those pieces of plastic. And I recognized my ignorance and carelessness about what actually happened to the plastic waste I was responsible for. It broke my heart. The numbness I'd been experiencing about the near-total degradation of our natural world thawed in an instant. The pain, the sorrow, the loss – all the emotions that we would naturally feel if we were tuned in to our interconnectedness with nature as we witness its demise – washed through me. I let it come, aware that I was experiencing an unusually powerful response, and as I did so, the emotions changed from grief to anger. I felt outraged, incensed by our failure to honour nature and her creations. How could we, as a species that knows how to love and care, have let this happen? How could we be inflicting such suffering on these wild, magnificent beings? And how were the plastic producers getting away with it?

I felt outraged, incensed by our failure to honour nature and her creations.

After some time, the anger gave way to a crystalline sense of resolve. I knew I needed to help the albatross in some way, and to do something about the plastic in our oceans. But where to begin? I wasn't making any inroads into mainstream TV presenting, my current employer wasn't able to help, and after doing some research and firing off a few emails to organizations that were beginning to tackle plastic pollution, I drew a blank. No one was hiring, so whatever I did to support any charities would be voluntary. That was OK, but I didn't really just want to raise money for them doing a sponsored something or other; I wanted to create something that would raise awareness and make a difference.

Randomly, I ended up settling on an idea for a music video. Because if you're going to change the world, what better way to do it than through a song? Er, right? I dabble in music, and a few months earlier I had written a heartfelt song called 'Burden', about cultivating the energy to transform our inner daily stresses and struggles. I had an idea that, if set to a video about plastic pollution, the lyrics would transpose to the feeling I now had … and with luck it would go viral and all the young-sters around the world would be inspired to stop drinking from single-use plastic bottles and those companies would all go out of business and a few squillion tonnes of bottle caps would stop washing up in the Great Pacific Gyre and the albatross mummies and daddies would stop mistaking them for fish and stop feeding them to their chicks and all would be well. Or so I thought. And I was going to need money to make it all happen.

A wake-up call, or a sense that you want to do more good, isn't always a soul-shaking, spine-tingling experience. Timing played an important factor in mine. I was at home, alone, when I saw that video. Had I been on a busy train or bus, or at work, I wouldn't have had the freedom to feel and express what came up. My eyes would have watered, I'd probably have thought 'how awful', and perhaps carried on scrolling. Numbness to the scale and seriousness of the social and environmental crisis we face today is part self-defence, part overwhelm and part inertia. Sometimes it takes a whopping great yank on the heartstrings to break that spell. At other times, it's the steady drips of information that, like the river wearing down the rock, gradually reveal our calling.

The crowdfunder

I'd never run a crowdfunding campaign, and by 2014 there were a couple of platforms to choose from. I went with Crowdfunder, which had the personal service I was looking for. (I needed help to set it up, and Crowdfunder was able to give me that.) I did the pitch video with the film crew I was planning to hire if my Crowdfunder was successful, set up my rewards (what people get in return for supporting your project financially) and pressed 'publish'. I was off. For the four weeks, as well as having a full-time job, my mission was to raise £5,000 ($8,500) – to cover the costs of the crowdfunder film, song production and music video – from friends, family, colleagues and local businesses. I figured I could probably only raise around £500 ($850) from friends and family, so as part of the rewards I built in a sponsorship package, whereby any business or corporate that donated £500 would get its logo at the end of the video and be invited to the launch party.

The first week was a blur, with money kerchinging into the pot every hour. I printed out little invitations and took them to green networking events, fired off emails and blasted my social media channels and mailing list.

It was fast-paced and exciting, and by the end of the first week I'd raised £2,000 ($3,500). Result! I felt it was going to be a breeze. But in the second week, everything went quiet. My networks had all heard about it and the launch had gen-erated lots of excitement, but now the buzz had become faint background noise. My Crowdfunder mentor told me this was normal, that the first week often brings the biggest flurry of activity, then things go quiet for the middle two weeks before picking up again in the last week. But I'd raised just 20 per cent of my target, and the lack of donations during the second week, despite my efforts to keep the content going, was worrying. By the end of that week I'd managed to bring in another £500, but was still only halfway, with just a week to go and my networks already tapped.

I started to stress out big-time. Failure wasn't an option, since at that point with Crowdfunder if you didn't reach your full target, you wouldn't receive any of the donations. I didn't have a back-up plan or savings to put in to get it over the line. My friend and flatmate at the time, however, had an ace up her sleeve. She introduced me to one of Bristol's super-connected, super-bright changemakers, Zoe Sear. At the time, Zoe was head of the mayor's office, so she was probably *the* best-connected, most influential woman in town. I was nervous at our meeting, fully aware of her power to make my campaign a success, if she wanted to. I was also aware that she was intensely busy and doing really important things all day long, so I wasn't sure that asking her for help so I could make a music video was going to hold much weight. But 'If you don't ask, you don't get' is one of my mantras, so I told Zoe about the plight of the albatross in the Midway Islands and my intention to make a music video that would help. Amazingly, she got it. After a half-hour speed meeting, she said to leave it with her, and that she'd find me four sponsors by the end of the week. I remember crying tears of relief when she walked away. With her help, I felt I might just do it.

Sure enough, within a week Zoe had magicked up (or pretty much commanded) four businesses, all aligned with my mission, to donate £500 each. Thanks to her, I hit my target in week three, and raised an extra £1,000 ($1,750) stretch target in the last week, giving me a total of £6,000 ($10,250) to fulfil my project. We'd done it!

For more practical advice and tips on crowdfunding and fundraising, go to page 127.

Turning the tide

While the song and video were in production – a slow process – I worked on what might come next. And, thanks to my being in the right place at the right time one morning, that came as a shocking experience of the plastic pollution problem, this time on my doorstep.

I was cycling to Pilates with my then partner, Gus, and spotted something unusual in the river. We got off our bikes to have a closer look, and I couldn't believe my eyes: there were islands of plastic floating downstream. The Severn Estuary, of which the River Avon is part, has the second-highest tidal range in the world, which means we get some huge surges, especially when it's a spring tide (confusingly, those happen twice a month, not just in spring). While Bristolians were marvelling at the high tide upstream in the harbour, we were witnessing a massive purge of

… there were islands of plastic floating downstream

plastic from the city, out to sea. Hundreds of plastic bottles and carrier bags were caught up in these floating clumps of litter, muddy sticks and leaves. My inner TV presenter ever at the ready, I grabbed my phone and asked Gus to film me so we could document and share it. The footage came out pretty well, despite the awful sound, and it got thousands of views on YouTube and even made the local news. (It ended up getting more views than my music video, quite possibly making more of an impact ... and cost me nothing. Lol.)

Here I was, in the current 'European Green Capital', seeing tonnes of plastic spewing out of the city. I was stunned. While I was certain – or, shall we say, naïvely optimistic – that my music video was going to help, after seeing those scenes I wanted to check in more with my home city and see what the hell was going on with our own litter problem. I mean, if we, the reigning Green Capital of Europe with all our 'zero-waste to landfill' accolades, couldn't sort it out, what hope was there for the majority world countries without waste collection and recycling infrastructure? Something other than the new, localized resolve to 'sort out our own shit' had come to me on the outgoing tide that morning. So had the name of this project I was inadvertently creating: City to Sea.

I still had a full-time job in TV, but the energy I'd put into the fundraising campaign had built a wave of momentum and I wanted to harness it. I connected with Livvy Drake, a plastics activist living in Bristol, and we decided to organize community workshops to find out why the plastic problem was so bad in the city, who cared about it and what we could do about it. The turnout was awesome; awareness of the problem was growing and so was the sense of urgency to make changes. We decided to share our findings with a wider audience on live TV (there had to be some perks to my day job), to see if we could mobilize some action.

When I realized I wasn't Adele

I launched the music video on World Oceans Day, 8 June 2015. My boss at Made in Bristol TV had kindly agreed to let me host an hour-long live panel discussion on plastic pollution, broadcast from the prestigious Watershed arts centre. We had some stellar experts on the panel, a beautiful exhibition of art made from marine plastic, and a shiny new City to Sea logo. The production team was fantastic and it was a stonking success.

Now all that needed to happen was for millions of people to watch the video, download the song and stop using single-use plastic. I sent the link everywhere I could think of: my Crowdfunder supporters, my networks, local radio stations … But two weeks after launching the video, it had had only about 2,000 views on YouTube. Yikes. I was getting great feedback, but it wasn't getting the traction I felt it needed in order to have the impact I was hoping for. The money I'd raised for my chosen charity came to a grand total of £17.68 ($27.60). I'd raised £6,000 to produce the song and the video, and was beginning to wonder if I shouldn't just have raised that money for the charity instead. Had I indulged in a massive vanity project and totally missed the point? I mean, it's not as though I was Adele, an established megastar with tens of millions of followers and fans. I mused on these things for a while, but after a healthy amount of soul-searching and delving into my conscience, motives and intention, I decided I'd done the right thing. A journey of a thousand miles starts with a single step, and even though that single step hadn't been a hit single, it was a start, and I wasn't planning on stopping.

My resolve was unsinkable. The albatross were still dying, my city's river was still pumping out plastic, and my new relationship with the sea was bouying me up with a constant source of energy and inspiration.

The transition

The community events we'd run, as well as the live broadcast, had shown us that the three main offenders when it came to plastic pollution in Bristol were single-use drinks bottles, plastic cotton buds (Q-tips) and storm drains. The last – those gaps at the side of roads that swallow up rain surges (and also tonnes of plastic litter) and divert them into the nearest river – felt like a re-engineering feat that was beyond even my outrageous optimism. The other two felt like something we could have a crack at. We'd discovered through our workshops that no NGOs or local community groups were working on the plastic problem in Bristol, and none planned to. Local groups had started running riverbank clean-ups, but no one was tackling the source of the problem. And none of the local marine conservation groups or charities had the resources or funding to take it on. If we wanted to fix it, we'd have to do it ourselves.

After some toing and froing with the company that was running the Green Capital initiatives, we managed to secure a grant of £11,000 ($17,200) for our first campaign, Refill. The idea was simple: connect Bristolians to the thousands of taps available in shops and cafes across the city, and maybe get more water fountains installed, to encourage people to refill their water bottles instead of buying bottled water. Livvy's behaviour-change research at our events had identified a couple of barriers to this: remembering to carry your bottle with you; and feeling embarrassed to ask for a free refill in a shop. By creating a bright, visual invitation to passers-by, through posters and stickers in the window, and a digital map of Refill Stations, we could break down those barriers and help people feel relaxed about getting a free top-up. Meanwhile, down in Bude, Cornwall, another community water-refill initiative was getting going, raising funds for the local sea pool. They said we could use their brilliant posters and, not wanting to duplicate, we graciously accepted.

I decided to set up a steering group, a group of advisors and experts willing to give their time free of charge to support our work (for more on that, see page 145). I invited eight of Bristol's leading lights – either experts in marine conservation and environmental issues or 'super-connectors' to help us further our mission – to form an advisory panel. Although I was still massively uneducated on race and diversity, I knew I didn't want a typically white, male, middle-class steering group, so I made sure it was more representative from the get-go: 50 per cent female and 25 per cent People of Colour. They were a phenomenal bunch of academics, scientists, communicators and collaborators, and I was bowled over by their willingness to support us, for free.

I still had a full-time job and was building up City to Sea in my spare time, but the initial funding was now enabling two people – Livvy and Gus – to do good and get paid for two days a week. I started to think we might be on to something. The Refill campaign was a huge success and we started getting enquiries from other counties, cities and individuals wanting to run their own scheme. Through work, I'd met another plastic campaigner, Michelle Cassar. As well as having an impressive track record (possibly world record) at living without single-use plastic, she was a talented photographer and wanted to get into filmmaking. We bonded over our passion for sorting out the seas, and Michelle started volunteering on Refill. So now we were four, and I was getting increasingly itchy feet in my day job.

I wanted to leave TV and put all my energy into City to Sea, because I felt we had an opportunity to scale up the Refill campaign. I also wanted to tackle the cotton-bud problem. It had been almost a year since I started my crowdfunding campaign and I began to spend all my free time on City to Sea, and juggling that on top of my intensely demanding TV job was starting to take its toll. But I'd not yet got City to Sea to a place where it could support me and the others financially. Some 15 years after my lucrative recruitment days, I was earning a good enough salary (around £35,000/$55,000) through my TV job. But if I kept doing the TV work, I wouldn't be able to put in the hours City to Sea needed to succeed. The decision I'd been wrestling with was made simpler by my employer, when I was made redundant. Funding for local TV had dried up, the channel wasn't making any money and they needed to make big cuts. So I was free to make a go of City to Sea, and I'd have to make it snappy because I had rent to pay, a son to support, and no savings.

Actually, the son part was probably my saving grace for the next few months. I'm not ashamed to admit that the first thing I did as a single parent was to sign up for housing benefit and tax credits, which would cover my rent. My dad disapproved, but I knew I wasn't 'scrounging off the state'; I was leaning into my government to support me while I built something that could ultimately save them money (the UK government spends almost £700 million/$920 million a year cleaning litter from the streets and countryside), not to mention produce the wider global benefits of stopping plastic from destroying the biodiversity of our oceans. To reboot my income, I re-established my freelance presenter and journalist portfolio. It was tight, and with an annual income of around £15,000 ($23,500), 'frugal' was my middle name. But I was free to do the work I was being called to do, so I threw myself into it, not realizing I'd inadvertently chosen the deep end.

Our first big campaign win

The money came in slowly. So slowly, in fact, that we almost didn't make it. We all had to get other work to supplement our City to Sea income, and we all put in extra hours for free to get things off the ground. I researched

The money came in slowly. So slowly, in fact, that we almost didn't make it.

funders, water companies, corporates – anyone who had a stake in our rivers and seas – and pitched my arse off. I wangled my way (usually with a persuasive email or by finding a common connection) into industry meetings that were so ridiculously above my station that I had to pat myself on the back for my tenacity, or audacity. Eventually it started to pay off. We got a few thousand here, and a few thousand there – mostly from grants and sponsorship, and by the end of year one, four of us were being paid two days a week. I decided to set up City to Sea as a community interest company (CIC), meaning we'd have 'non-profit' status without the paperwork and possible restrictions of a charity. (For more on organizational structures, go to page 107.)

We started winning awards, including £50,000 ($65,000) of software development time for an app for Refill, along with an £11,000 ($15,000) cash grant from the prestigious Geovation fund – a huge morale boost and a welcome three months' pay for us. I spent most of my time networking and filling in grant applications, while Gus beavered away on building up the network of Refill schemes across the UK, and Livvy and Michelle worked on their dance routines (actually very important stuff that made the headlines). One by one the water companies were getting interested in what we were up to, which was, essentially, making tap water sexy. I remember when our local water company, Bristol Water, became our first corporate sponsor after the success of Refill Bristol in 2015. Before I tapped them for funding, the customer services director's exact words were, 'They've created a knockout PR campaign that money couldn't buy.' I replied, obviously, 'Oh yes it can.' He couldn't refuse to give us some money after saying that.

And then #SwitchtheStick happened. I wanted to do something about the insane number of plastic cotton buds, or Q-tips for my American readers, washing up on the world's beaches. In the UK alone, about 180 million were being flushed down the toilet every day. Being so small, they pass through sewage filters and directly into our rivers and seas. There was no reason for cotton buds – a product we use for about 30 seconds before throwing it away – to be made out of a material that by design lasts for about 400 years. (Or, to be precise, that lasts forever, but once in the ocean – exposed to the sun's rays, salt and bashing waves – breaks down into tiny microplastics that float around in the ocean, absorbing toxic chemicals that have run off into the sea from polluting intensive agriculture, to be eaten by fish that mistake that yummy-looking fragment of plastic for food, at which point the toxins pass into the fish, either making it sick or making us sick when we eat the fatty bits of fish that have accumulated the nasties. And that's if the larger pieces of plastic aren't mistaken by a bird for a fish and end up in its stomach, causing death by starvation or perforation. You get the picture.) Cotton buds could surely be made from cardboard, as in the good old days, and at least then if they *were* flushed (which they shouldn't be, but if they *were* …) they would swell up and therefore be too big to pass through the sewage filters or, if they did escape, would quickly biodegrade.

In the UK alone, about 180 million [cotton buds] were being flushed down the toilet every day

But I had no idea how to run a campaign. What do you do when you don't know where to begin? Phone a friend. Or, in my case, ask someone on my steering group. Thomas Bell had worked as a campaign manager for the Marine Conservation Society and had run numerous successful campaigns on ocean pollution, beach cleans and marine conservation zones, so he was the perfect person to learn from. We met for coffees and planning sessions, scoped things out and made a plan. Now all I needed was money – about £45,000 ($60,000) of it.

It made sense to start by asking the water companies if they'd fund the campaign, since the plastic buds were not only spewing out of their sewers and causing them negative PR, but were also a major factor in sewage blockages. These little plastic sticks were joining forces with masses of baby wipes (also mostly made of plastic, also shouldn't be flushed in the first place) and menstrual products (ditto) in the sewers and – I hope you're not eating your lunch right now – coagulating with fats, oils and greases that had been poured down the sink (instead of going into the bin or the compost) to form massive 'fatbergs', some of them 80 metres (260 ft) long. Removing fatbergs was costing the water industry about £100 million ($132 million) a year, and, according to them, cotton-bud sticks were a major culprit. So £45,000 didn't seem a big ask if I was going to make a dent in that.

I discovered that representatives from each water company met four times a year to discuss 'sewage network abuse' – in other words, how to stop people flushing down the toilet stuff other than pee, paper and poo. I persuaded them to allow us to present in their next meeting, and brought Thomas along for credibility, which I was grateful for, as it became clear pretty quickly that these people weren't impressed by a 'nobody' with no track record other than a failed music video and a then small-scale tap-water campaign. Still, requesting about £5,000 (£6,500) from each water company was pretty small fry, and I felt confident in our campaign plan, so I assumed they'd all bite my hand off when I offered to tackle their very sticky problem.

The meeting was tense and I was shitting myself, this being my first official 'pitch' in a boardroom in more than 15 years.

Only three out of ten companies said yes. My saviours. City to Sea didn't have the credentials to give the rest the confidence that we could pull this off. That £15,000 ($19,500) was a fraction of what we thought we needed to deliver the campaign. It was time to get creative.

I called a filmmaker buddy with whom I'd done lots of freelance presenting, shot a campaign video in a day calling on the nine major UK supermarkets to 'Switch the Stick' from plastic to paper, set up a web page and started blasting it around to our supporters and social media followers, of which we had around 2,000. In a month or so we had about six thousand signatures on our petition, which wasn't bad for an organization that had been going – officially – for only six months. It caught the attention of the burgeoning petition platform 38 Degrees, which suggested I run my petition via their website to increase its visibility and get more signatures. That proved a very wise decision. Within a month of launching it on the 38 Degrees platform, we had an extra 150,000 signatures, which, back in 2016, was pretty exciting. So many people were threatening to take their business elsewhere that the supermarkets were starting to listen.

I'd also managed to wangle (you're starting to see 'wangling' as a theme in my skillset now, aren't you) my way into a meeting with the sustainability leads from all the UK supermarkets – a massive moment of imposter syndrome. Whenever I get that 'who the hell am I to be telling these people what to do?' feeling, I take a moment to check myself. I take a breath or five and remind myself that I'm not there for me, but for the oceans and all the marine wildlife that isn't represented in the room. That usually frees me from the nets of self-concern and makes me show up for the bigger picture. Anyway, that meeting went well and I felt particularly pleased that I'd been able to ask them nicely if they'd switch the stick, before whacking them all over the proverbial head if they didn't.

Working with 38 Degrees was a blast, and one by one the super-markets came on board. Michelle and I – paying ourselves two days a week to run the campaign – would dance on the tables every time we got an email from a retailer, ticking off our hit list and tallying up the millions of plastic cotton buds we'd be stopping from getting into our oceans. When there was just one remaining, Wilko, we honed the laser beam of 156,000 engaged online activists and blasted its

Whenever I get that 'who the hell am I to be telling these people what to do?' feeling, I take a moment to check myself.

social media channels. We felt a teeny bit bad that its '12 Days of Christmas' campaign was completely ruined, as every single thing Wilko posted on social media was hijacked by hundreds of outraged #SwitchtheStick supporters. Eventually it caved in, probably just to shut us all up. It was the week before Christmas and we'd done it. All nine UK supermarkets had agreed to switch permanently to paper stems the following year, a move that would stop more than two billion cotton buds – that's around 420 tonnes of non-recyclable, single-use plastic – from being produced, and potentially flushed, every year.

We'd had our first big campaign win on a budget of £15,000 and increased our mailing list from 2,000 to 20,000. We were very, very ready for the Christmas holidays.

For more on campaigning, see page 164.
For more on fundraising, see page 120.

Making up a number, then tripling it

We'd made a name for ourselves among our fans, followers, press and peers, so getting funding was easier in 2017 than in the previous year. I realized pretty quickly that, without a dedicated fundraising person, which we couldn't afford yet, grant funding wouldn't bring in enough cash to enable the four of us to put food on the table, and corporate partnerships – mostly at this stage through UK water companies – seemed to be getting more results. Taking advice from a fundraising friend who'd founded his own non-profit, I decided to build up City to Sea with a diverse income stream of corporate partners, grants and foundations, and individual donors. We'd later add product partners to that mix.

I went back to the water companies with a proposal to tackle plastic pollution from baby wipes and period products. Michelle and I had smashed #SwitchtheStick on a £15,000 budget and were in a much stronger position to persuade them to power our next campaign. They'd been really impressed with our work and were keen to support us, so this time our request for about £60,000 ($80,000) for a year-long programme was successful. We'd budgeted for three days a week each plus campaign expenses and I felt, for the first time, that we had a real shot at making this thing – whatever it was – a success.

Meanwhile, Gus was tearing his hair out single-handedly growing the Refill campaign. It was a slog; mobilizing volunteers and signing up new schemes were relatively easy, because we were getting dozens of requests each week for new schemes, but the app was time-consuming and fundraising impossibly slow. By this point we'd managed to get four water companies to fund Refill communities in their local area, and it was working: people were switching from plastic water bottles to reusables and public perception of tap water was on the up. Demand was there but our capacity wasn't, and we couldn't get the buy-in we needed from the water companies to enable us to scale. Two years in we were overworked, underfunded and starting to show signs of burnout.

Then, one morning, an email landed in my inbox that changed our lives completely. Water UK, the industry body for water companies, was enquiring how it would look, and how much it would cost, to scale the Refill campaign nationally. I nearly fell off my chair. In fact, I think I cried. Finally someone had noticed what we were doing and wanted to help. We worked up a two-year proposal, thinking it would probably cost around £100,000 ($130,000) a year, and ran it past a few people for feedback. All was looking good until I grabbed half an hour with Craig, the new CEO of the Wave, which had generously been letting us work in its office for free for two years. (Another key factor in us being able to do stuff on a shoestring.) He scanned the proposal and proceeded to give me what was probably the most game-changing piece of advice I've ever had: 'Nat, you need to triple this.' Craig had watched us limping along, albeit impactfully, for months and could see that we were massively undervaluing ourselves, as well as massively underestimating the work it would take to deliver a truly sustainable, legacy campaign. 'Not only do you need to triple it, you need it for three years, not two, so ask for a million.' My head was spinning and I was laughing out loud. Me? Ask for a million pounds? I could almost hear a glass ceiling shattering above my head. 'One millllion dollars!' I replied in my best Dr Evil voice, lifting my little finger to my mouth. Craig took me through the proposal, showing me the gaps and grilling me on the deliverables. By the end of the half hour, I believed him. And I believed in myself and our campaign and what we needed to make it happen.

Those 30 minutes of free advice resulted in us receiving triple the amount I was planning to ask for. After many meetings and much toing and froing on the numbers, the plan and its impact, we secured a contract of about £300,000 ($390,000) a year for two years. It wasn't a million, and it wasn't for three years, but it was enough to cause a seismic shift in our operations.

Craig was right, of course. To do what we did over those two years (which eventually became three, because we were doing a great job) and get the Refill campaign to the point it's at today, we needed every penny – and then some. But the real beauty of securing significant funding is that it instils confidence in other funders. We were now a trusted, professional campaigning organization, and doors were starting to open.

For more on allies, mentors and advisors, see page 146.

Building the ship while sailing in it

We grew from five to twelve staff almost overnight, packed like sardines in our little corner of the Wave's office (which we were now paying desk rent for – I couldn't scrounge after Craig's part in our recent success). A few months later we moved – with the Wave, which was also about to explode with staff – to a new office in a beautiful art-deco-meets-industrial building on Bristol's Floating Harbour. Over the past couple of years I'd imagined us having an office by the water, so that we could connect even more to our mission and enjoy sparkling sunny walks together instead of meeting in boardrooms.

The next two years were fast-paced, with more highs than lows. I'd promoted Rebecca Burgess, our super-talented, promising partnerships manager, to CEO at the end of 2018 and felt ready to hand over the reins to her while I focused on giving talks, doing media and writing my book *How to Save the World for Free* (2019). Apparently it was unusual for a founder to slide over from the captain's seat, but I'd had almost four years at the helm and was more than happy to let someone else steer for a while. She had a completely different business skillset from me, with a background in commercial partnerships and experience working at large charities, and she was hungry for it. She increased the team to 25 over her two years in the role, restructuring the organization, winning awards and generally rocking at her first CEO job, aged 34.

Generally, though, we were winging it. I'd never run a campaigning organization, Rebecca had never been CEO, the chair of our board had never been a chairperson and none of the people on our team had experience of working for an organization of this kind. Perhaps that is why we did things differently, made a name for ourselves and got results. And also why we learned things the hard way, worked too hard and got things wrong. But since I never anticipated any of this, I've never felt too attached to the outcome. Obviously I want our campaigns and app to stop as much single-use plastic from getting into our oceans as possible. And I want our team of talented, passionate and genuinely awesome people to have opportunities for a good career and salary at City to Sea. But when I first felt the urge to do something to help those ridiculously cute albatross chicks,

We grew from five to twelve staff almost overnight

I could never have predicted that it would lead to this. Every month has felt like an adventure, and every month that we do good and get paid has been a blessing. And what do you do when you're feeling blessed? Pass it on.

For more on roles, responsibilities and building teams, see page 148.

Sharing is caring

I spent a large part of the summer of 2020 on furlough (the UK government's scheme to support businesses during the COVID-19 pandemic). We'd had a couple of major funders drop out as a result of the pandemic, and some of our campaigns had to be paused or cancelled, so we decided to furlough as many people as possible without compromising our output. Single-use plastic was making a comeback through PPE and hand sanitizer, and we played a leading role in pushing back against the plastics industry, which was seizing the moment around the world to reverse plastic bans and progress in the refill and reuse space.

The summer I had away from the front line felt like a much-needed sabbatical. I'd finally managed to buy my own house, so I spent my time nesting and resting, doing DIY, and making sure I switched off. Although Rebecca had been taking the strain of running City to Sea, my schedule over the last couple of years had been demanding; I was travelling all over the UK and Europe giving talks, and was rarely home for more than a few days at a time. I'd developed a digestive condition, a hiatus hernia, back in 2017, and through my research (and reading Dr Gabor Maté's book *When the Body Says No*) had realized it was stress-related. I needed a break and, as a side effect of the unfolding pandemic, I got it through furlough.

It's tempting to skip over this part as indulgent. But it's important, because burnout is a real and common thing among activists and campaigners – even more so than business leaders. Being engaged in a battle we may never win is tiring, and unless we actively prioritize self-care and regeneration, it can overwhelm us. As I found, taking a step back and switching off can be exactly what's needed for you to replenish your reserves, refine your focus and rekindle your mojo.

Pretty much every week over the last couple of years, I'd received at least one email from someone asking me for help. About half were plastic activists who wanted advice on starting up a campaign or getting funding; the other half were people who wanted to get something going – a new business, charity or environmental campaign. With my relentless schedule I'd never been able to offer more than a quick reply with a few suggestions. But after a few weeks of proper rest and a more spacious diary, I was able to say yes. I started giving weekly mentoring sessions to two brilliant women who were starting up an organization called the Launchpad Collective, training refugees to be ready to work in the UK. I also supported Flight Free UK as an advisor and helped a friend on her organic farm. But if there was only one of me, and if my diary became full again (which it did as I stepped back into the CEO role in early 2021), it wasn't clear how I could maintain this or, more importantly, scale it. I wanted to be able to answer as many questions as I could, I wanted to share knowledge with others and I wanted to help build a movement. You can probably guess, given you're reading this, that writing a book was one way I thought I could do that.

So that's where I'll leave my founder's journey and tales from the coyote trail of my career path. Now it's time to get down to business, and focus on the practical steps you might need to take on your way to doing good and getting paid.

For more on looking after yourself and avoiding burnout, see page 192.

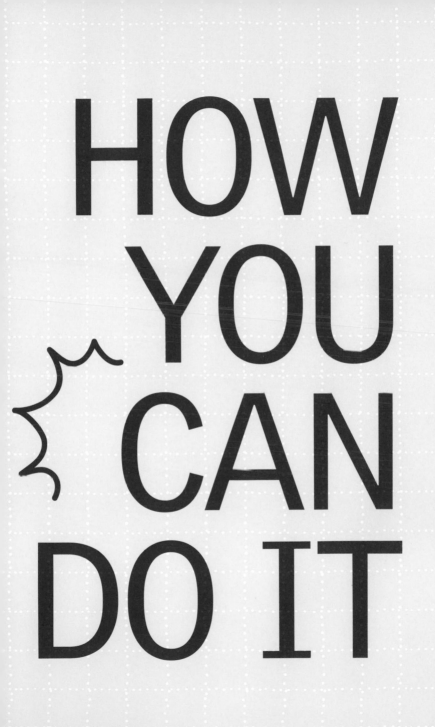

YOU

Before you commit to starting something new, it's a good idea to get a fresh sense of your foundations: what you're building on, what resources you have and what your strengths are. This can make the difference between keeping your project physically, emotionally and financially sustainable, and crashing and burning after a few months. If you know you want to do good but aren't sure exactly *what* you want to do, the tools in this chapter will help you find clarity. You may also find this chapter helpful when it comes to understanding the people you work with, or when you're hiring and building a team.

STRENGTHS, SKILLS AND SWEET SPOTS

Let's start with your strengths. What are you personally good at? You might have a sense already, but personality assessments or psychometric tests are fantastic tools for developing awareness of and confidence in your superpowers. They help you identify your strengths and play to them, rather than worrying about your weaknesses. For example, you might thrive with order and love geeking out on spreadsheets, or you might be impulsive, flexible and intuitive. Knowing yourself helps you believe in yourself, and that's an essential ingredient for success. Here's an overview of four of the most common personality tests, starting with my favourite, which – helpfully – is also the least expensive.

CliftonStrengths Assessment™

Formerly known as the Clifton StrengthsFinder and named after its inventor, the US psychologist Don Clifton, this 45-minute online questionnaire uses 177 questions to help you identify the 'true you'. The creators claim that their personalized reports and pool of resources will help you to 'turn talents into strengths' and maximize your potential. I'd have to agree with them. Although you might get a bit of a sweat on doing it, because you're against the clock – you have just 20 seconds to answer each question, so there's no time to overthink.

Once you've taken the test, your talents are categorized into 34 themes. These are divided into four 'domains': strategic thinking, relationship building, influencing and executing. You receive a customized report to help you understand your profile, play to your strengths and manage potential weaknesses, and a guide to help you chart your future course. Gallup, which operates the assessment, claims that those who do the test are six times more engaged with their jobs, six times more likely to agree strongly that they have the opportunity to do what they do best every day, and three times more likely to say they have an excellent quality of life. All for £20/$20. (You can pay more – £50/$50 – to unlock the full 34 themes, but I found just the top five themes enough.) In terms of learning about my strengths, it's the best £20 I've ever spent, and that's why we use it at City to Sea.

Myers-Briggs

The Myers-Briggs Type Indicator® (MBTI) personality assess-ment is based on research by the renowned psychologist Carl Jung and claims to be the world's most popular; it's used two million times a year. Created by the daughter-mother power duo Isabel Myers and Katharine Briggs, it has 70 years of research behind it and is used by psychologists and counsellors, and also in the workplace, usually within an HR department, to help managers understand what makes people tick.

The MBTI creators say that identifying your personality type through the test helps you to learn what role it plays in your mental and physical well-being, allows you to grow as an individual by understanding how you learn best and move forward on your ideas, and enables you to build stronger, more successful connections at work, at home and pretty much everywhere else. It's broken down into two steps: Step 1 identifies personality type (there are 16 in this system) and motivations and how we interact with the world around us; Step 2 goes into more detail about the Step 1 preferences. It supposedly 'hits at the heart of who someone is' and 'helps you to understand the DNA of someone's personality'.

It can be done online for around $50 (£36) at mbtionline .com and also takes about 45 minutes, or you can take a deep dive via myersbriggs.org with a trained consultant, coach or therapist. If time and money are of the essence, there are loads of free '16 personalities' quizzes online that can give you a quick result. Just make sure you do a few, as the results of these free tests vary.

DISC

Used by about a million people a year to improve teamwork, communication and productivity in the workplace, DISC is a super-helpful, powerful and insightful tool. Originally developed by William Moulton Marston, a physiological psychologist with a PhD from Harvard, DISC describes four main personality profiles: (D)ominance, (I)nfluence, (S)teadiness and (C)onscientiousness. The idea is that for an effective team and successful business you need a good cross section of those personalities.

We dabbled pretty successfully with DISC at City to Sea, and found that, like CliftonStrengths, it helped us to learn more about communication styles, to understand each other and to respect each other's ways of working. If you're building a team, this a great tool to use. If it's just you, CliftonStrengths is probably sufficient. The DISC online assessment costs $72 (£52) and is available via lots of websites.

Talent Dynamics

This test is aimed more at entrepreneurs, but I found it equally helpful to learn about my working styles whether I was working for myself or for another organization. Talent Dynamics can empower you as an activist, innovator or leader, because it helps you to identify the stuff you suck at. Its creator, Roger Hamilton, claims there are eight paths to wealth but only one that suits each person. By discovering your natural talents, you can identify the most fruitful path for you – usually the path of least resistance.

If you've got cash to invest in your development from the start, the $97 (£71) investment for Talent Dynamics is worth it. In return you receive a 36-page report, a training guide and a 'Learning Mission', and you'll feel more confident in your ability to follow your flow and do your best work. I also like the slightly esoteric nature of this test, which may come from the fact that at least some of its roots are in the I Ching.

LIVING YOUR BEST LIFE DOING YOUR BEST WORK

Once you've got clarity about your natural talents and strengths, work out what you actually *love* doing. Get it down on paper, ideally referring to the results of your personality profile, but, if you prefer, making an intuitive list of what you enjoy doing, not just what you're good at. (Although the two often go hand in hand, as we feel rewarded when we're doing work we're good at.) Ultimately, you're working towards finding the sweet spot of feeling good, doing good and getting paid: living your best life doing your best work. Let's go through a simple framework – one that you might be familiar with already – the Purpose Venn Diagram, created by the Spanish astrologer and author Andrés Zuzunaga in 2011. Since then it's been merged (possibly misappropriated) with the Japanese concept of *ikigai* (from *iki*, meaning 'life', and *gai*, meaning 'reason or benefit'), which is all about feeling that your work makes a difference in people's lives and is the not-so-secret sauce for longevity, happiness and even good health.[8]

Take a few minutes to have a go at it. Grab some paper and write down the things you love doing. Like, *really* love doing.

That could be bouncing around to music, listening to podcasts, meeting new people, crocheting, spending time with animals, river swimming, playing with kids ... literally anything. Don't censor it, just let all your loves out.

Next, write down the things you are great at. These are probably different from the things you love, more skills-based. It might be communication, design, listening, problem-solving, building things, growing things, seeing things from another perspective, programming software ... whatever skills you've acquired through learning or that came naturally to you, and that you're so good at, it feels almost effortless.

Now write down what the world needs. Don't get too carried away with this – you could end up writing a book on it – just choose up to ten issues, injustices or offerings you think need addressing. You don't have to focus on what needs fixing. For example, if the world had no music or art, it'd be a very sad place to be.

Now it's time to make the magic happen

Finally, write down what you are paid for. List the things you're currently earning from, your sources of income, as well as the things you *could* charge for. You might also want to ask yourself which jobs or positions light you up when you think of doing them.

Now it's time to make the magic happen by placing all that in the purpose framework. Essentially, the sweet spot is where these things overlap or intersect. Your purposeful work – doing good and getting paid – sits in the centre. If you can weave the threads together from what you love, what you're great at, what the world needs and what you can get paid for, you'll be setting yourself, and the world, up for something special.

Oh, and don't worry if you haven't worked out how to get paid yet. We'll come to that soon.

YOU LOVE IT

PASSION

MISSION

YOU ARE
GREAT AT IT

✳

THE WORLD
NEEDS IT

PROFESSION

VOCATION

YOU ARE
PAID FOR IT

✳ PURPOSE

ENERGY, TIME AND MONEY

Next, get a grasp of your resources, from how much time and energy you have to devote to your idea, to how much you can afford to spend on it. Whether you're looking to get a job in an existing organization or start something new, the following questions will help you to build the foundations for success and keep focused on your goals. For example, if it's January now and you want to have a new job or launch a product or campaign in July – but you have a job already, so you'll need to fit it in at weekends – you'll need to plan your mission accordingly. If you don't currently have an income but have six months of living expenses in the bank, you'll be focused on bringing in some funding before that window closes. Take a moment to run through these questions and see what resources you've got to play with.

Where are you at?

✱ How much time am I willing to commit daily/weekly?

✱ What blockers are there to me having more time, and can I remove any of them?

✱ How do I want my days to look?

✳ For how many months can I financially sustain myself before I need to get paid?

✳ Am I happy to do an internship, and if so, for how long?

✳ How much do I need to get paid?

✳ How much do I want to get paid?

✳ What non-financial resources do I have to support me? (Family, friends, neighbours, mailing list, social media followers, mentors and so on)

✳ How are my energy levels and how good am I at sustaining them under pressure?

✳ What tools or practices do I know to keep me energized?

If you are starting a business:

✳ How much start-up capital do I have to work with?

✳ How much risk am I happy to take?

✳ Am I willing to work with a venture capital firm or investors?

Keep the answers in a dedicated folder on your computer, or in a journal on your desk, so that you can keep coming back to them over the next year or so. Once you've got a good grasp of your capacity and resources, you can make a strategy for success that matches how much energy, time and money you have to nurture your mission.

YOUR MISSION

We've tackled the inner stuff – what makes you tick and how long you can keep ticking for – so now it's time to shift our focus to the task itself: your mission.

Do your research

Before you invest in a new project, campaign, website or business, scope out the landscape and see who's already working in that space. It's slightly different for businesses, since it's normal for most to have competitors, but when it's a campaign or links to a wider movement, you should check that you're not duplicating someone else's work. There may be someone like you out there who's a few steps ahead, and who desperately needs help.

When I embarked on the #SwitchtheStick campaign, I couldn't find any other organizations working on the issue. When I spoke to the supermarkets, before launching the petition, they'd not been contacted about it. So I powered ahead. Then someone showed me a news article about how the pharmaceutical company Johnson & Johnson had announced that it was going to phase out plastic cotton buds and switch to cardboard stems. This was attributed to a small but mighty charity called FIDRA, based in Scotland. After a mild panic

(How had I missed them? Could we carry on with our campaign? Had I just wasted three months planning and funding?) I jumped on the phone to FIDRA's campaigns manager to see what we could do. Collaboration was my first instinct, but after a couple of weeks of toing and froing with their board, they decided not to collaborate with us and that, in this instance, several voices were better than one. As it turned out, our campaign, which focused on own-brand supermarket buds, worked successfully as a separate one. It could easily have gone the other way, though, and this was a good lesson for me to take more time to scope out the landscape and stakeholders before I dived in. Human resources and funding are precious and not to be wasted through the duplication of effort.

Work through the following questions to see if you need to create something new. This can also work for setting up a business.

START HERE

Does my idea exist out there already?

YES / **NO**

Is it awesome?

NO

Can I bring something new to the sector?

Can I do better without duplicating?

YES

YES

YES

Am I filling a hole in the market or providing a service not yet offered?

Can I help them or get a job with them?

NO

YES

YES

Brilliant! Go get 'em! Read on for ways to volunteer, get a job or internship with them.

Awesome! Better get cracking then! Head to page 89 to get clear on your vision and values.

KNOWING YOUR WHY AND YOUR WHO

Traci Lewis is the co-founder of Catalyse Change CIC, a UK-based social enterprise that aims to help girls and young women to develop sustainability skills and knowledge for 'healthy, happy and green' communities, careers and planet. She shares what she has learned from her journey setting up two social businesses over the past six years.

When I first started working for myself, I looked at my skills, what I could offer and where the market demand might be. However, I didn't get to the nuts and bolts of what my real purpose was for doing it; I was more focused on how I could make money out of my existing skillset, so I was thinking straight away about products and services. It's really important that you don't start with that! I dived straight in, set up Sustain-Live Consulting Ltd – a sustainability change agency – and soon afterwards launched my website and brand. Basically I made the rookie mistake of not first properly understanding why I was doing it and for whom. I initially thought it would be more profitable to focus on working with SMEs [small and medium-sized enterprises], even though my experience is with social enterprises and charities, which unsurprisingly have ended up being my main customers.

Catalyse Change CIC, which I set up a year later, was developed over a much longer period. My motivation came from a much deeper place of wanting to empower young women – I could see that they were facing problems with confidence and mental health, and I felt called to do something about it. Because I was already working in sustainability, and because we're facing an ecological and climate emergency, I wanted that to be a key part of our focus as well. So from the outset there was a clear sense of who I was working for and why. Working with young women was very new to me, so I did a lot of research by talking to clever and connected people who work in education, as well as sustainability. I focused on questions like, 'What's a good way to tackle this? Who needs to be involved? And who else do we need to speak to?' I also got a board of directors together from the outset – three other motivated women – so we had many discussions about our shared purpose and how we could create a compelling vision and mission around it.

Sustain-Live Consulting just never had the same strong foundations and identity behind it. In fact, during the pandemic, I pivoted the business entirely to focus on supporting other women who want to work for themselves, now under my own name and brand. However, it's taken more than five years to get here, whereas Catalyse Change, which took a lot longer to create, is now much stronger and more impactful as a result. My advice is to do the work at the outset. It will save you a lot of pain, time and money in the long run.

INSTAGRAM: @TRACILEWIS79

How to help an existing campaign or organization (and ideally get a job with them)

So, you've identified your idea, project or campaign, and discovered from your research that there are already some brilliant people or organizations working on the same mission. Ideally, you'd work for them, or with them, bringing your skills, talent and passion to the table. Without wanting to state the obvious, the first step is to see if there are any jobs going there. Look at their websites and company LinkedIn profiles, and have a look on online job listing sites such as conservationjobboard.com (in the USA) and ecojobs.com, environmentjob.co.uk (in the UK) or ethicaljobs.com.au (in Australia).

There's a job going – how do I get it?

✳ Make sure your CV is clear, succinct, visually appealing and relevant to the job you're applying for. If you've never done that role before, make sure your CV highlights all the transferable skills. And it should definitely not be more than two pages. Focus on content over design; I'd rather see all the information I need clearly laid out on one page than have two over-designed pages with lots of white space.

✳ Do your research on the organization: its campaigns, vision, mission, values and so on, and get really clear about what you love about them, and what you can bring that they don't already have. Read their recent tweets and blogs, and connect with potential future team members on LinkedIn to see what they're sharing and caring about.

✳ The cover letter is key. Again, one page is generally enough, but two is fine if what you're writing about is relevant. This is your one and only first impression, so make it count. Sell yourself, say why you think you're the right person for the role, give examples of your experience that are relevant to the job description and *check for typos*. Unless you're dyslexic or neurodiverse (which is a good thing to mention on your covering letter and/or CV), typos are a no-no, so

check, double-check, and then get a friend with a keen eye
to check again.

✳ Check that your social media channels and online presence are aligned with the values of the organization. For
instance, if you're applying to work for an organization
that campaigns against single-use plastic, it's wise not to
have lots of photos of you posing on the beach with a drink
in a plastic cup with a plastic straw. Just saying.

On the following page is an example of a covering letter that
got Jas Tribe a job as campaign manager when we weren't even
looking for one. She applied for a role that, for reasons not to
do with her, she didn't get. But her application was so strong
that I couldn't stop thinking about her being on the team, so
a few months later we created a role for her.

Dear Gus and the City to Sea Team,

Ref: Application for the Role of Southeast Regional Coordinator, Refill Campaign

I am a passionate and dynamic environmentalist with significant campaign management experience and a solutions-based attitude to life. I really believe that I am the perfect fit for the role with your visionary Refill Campaign, as I hope the following summary will demonstrate ...

NINE REASONS TO CHOOSE ME

1. I have a First Class Honours Degree in Environmental Science from Plymouth University and won a special award for my marine-based dissertation.

2. I am 100% committed to marine conservation and environmental protection, taking every opportunity to create sustainable change throughout my working life and in my own time.

3. I have worked on public outreach and citizen science initiatives with marine conservation NGOs such as the Marine Biological Association, the Manta Trust, the Cape Eleuthera Institute and Fin Fighters.

4. I co-founded and voluntarily manage the UK's only dedicated shark and ocean festival (SharkFest UK) and created an award-winning waste reduction programme at Plymouth University (UniCycle Projects).

5. I have direct experience and a strong track record in creating, managing and delivering environmental projects and events from start to finish, including: planning, budgeting, promotion, leading volunteers, delivery and reporting.

6. Over the past 10 years I have gained experience in recruiting, coordinating and maintaining momentum and fun with volunteers between the ages of 4 and 60 in a wide variety of settings.

7. I have an extensive and actively engaged network of contacts, a proven ability to build new relationships through shared interests, and strong networking and social media skills. This gives me a solid base to build a growing campaign upon! I believe that community engagement is vital for creating successful and long-lasting change, and this is one of the reasons I love the Refill campaign!

8. I am an excellent communicator, a confident presenter and comfortable in a leadership role, taking every opportunity to promote positive environmental and social change.

9. I am a fast learner, a determined worker and a creative thinker, and I feel confident that I can make a huge contribution to the work of the Refill campaign. I'm ready to dive in!

I have enclosed my full CV to support my application – but I would love to have an opportunity to discuss the job with you in person, so that I can expand further on my experience and suitability for this role.

Yours sincerely,

JASMINE TRIBE

There's no job going – how do I work with them?

Jas's example is one way you can get on people's radars, so never doubt that even if you're not successful the first time, you won't have made an impression. If there's no job going, here are a few tips to help you introduce yourself to the organization and get a foot in the door:

✳ Ask if you can volunteer with them. Generally, the people you're emailing will be really busy, so they need to know how you can help them, ideally in tangible ways. Taking on a volunteer can be time-consuming, so if you're really clear on your skills and how you can make this person's life/job easier, or amplify their impact, it'll be much more likely that they'll say yes. Let them know you've done your research, how much time you have to offer (even if it's just a couple of hours a week) and what problem they might be facing that you can help to solve. Again, a short, kick-ass covering email is key.

... a short, kick-ass covering email is key

✳ See if you can find a paid internship through a local university or sponsored programme. (Unpaid internships are one of the systemic barriers that limit the diversity of young workers; more on that on page 151.)

✳ Find sponsorship or a funding opportunity to pay for your role. For the most part, NGOs and non-profits are under-resourced and underfunded. The best thing for someone to come knocking at their door with is not just the skills, but also the resources to fund them. It's a good idea to get their blessing first, particularly if you're going to do something public-facing to raise funds. See page 120 for more on how to finance your idea.

✱ Be an advocate for their work or brand. If you know your way around social media, you can connect with your dream organization and its audience by sharing, commenting on and engaging with its posts – and creating your own. It might not mean they suddenly message you with a job offer, but it'll show you're already supporting and understanding the mission when and if a job arises, and that adds great value to your application. Start by following the organization on social media channels, and stay up to date with key milestones, campaigns and impact.

✱ Get out there, make connections and network. There's nothing like meeting some of the team in person if you can, and that goes for online conferences, too. You can always follow up with a LinkedIn message if you didn't get a chance to meet someone personally. Put in the time to be in the right place at the right time and introduce yourself.

Go forth and land your dream job (or, at least, a spot on a stepping stone nearer it). Remember that if – after doing your research, scoping out opportunities and trying to work for existing purpose-led businesses or charities – you still aren't getting paid to do good, you can absolutely, resolutely, do your own thing. Read on to find out where to begin.

RESOURCES

* On Purpose: onpurpose.org
* 80,000 Hours: 80000hours.org
* Simon Sinek, *Find Your Why*

GETTING STARTED

So, you've decided to do your own thing ... yay! This will be either because you can't get work in the field you're passionate about, or because you've discovered that the work being done in the field isn't enough for you, and you think you could add something valuable. You may have a new product or business idea and be looking to start your own purpose-driven company. Or perhaps you're a renegade maverick ready to heal some aspect of the world, and just want to get on with it.

Vision

To know where you're heading and what success looks like, and to be able to bring others on board, you need a guiding light, a North Star ... a vision. Your vision can be lofty, idealistic and exciting – it's what gets you out of bed in the morning eager to change the world. It will help you to pitch your idea and rally support, and ultimately it will keep you and everyone involved in your mission aligned, motivated and focused.

A Forbes study that looked at data from over 50,000 employees discovered that people who find their company's vision meaningful have average engagement scores of 68 per cent, compared to just 18 per cent for those who don't.[9] The study also found that 70 per cent of employees don't understand their company's vision at all. That's a huge number of unengaged people! So, while your vision must be aspirational, it should also make sense – to everyone. At City to Sea, ours is '*A world where everyone connects their actions to our oceans, so all life can thrive.*'

Here are more examples of vision statements from some of the world's leading purpose-led organizations, charities and brands:

Esusu, a mobile platform helping individuals mostly from marginalized communities to save money, access capital and build credit.
To unleash the power of data to bridge the racial wealth gap.

Patagonia, an American company that markets and sells outdoor clothing.
We're in business to save our home planet.

Choose Love, a global charity providing refugees and displaced people with everything from lifesaving search-and-rescue boats to food and legal advice.
A world that chooses love and justice every day, for everyone.

Numi Tea, a premium, Fair Trade sustainable company specializing in tea.
Our vision is to activate a chain of positivity and possibility that radiates far and wide. Through our products and practices, we create lasting positive change.

The Human Rights Campaign, the largest LGBTQ+ advocacy group and political lobbying organization in the USA.
Equality for everyone.

Thinx, a pioneering brand of period underwear.
Because every person with a period deserves peace of mind.

These examples show that your vision is not the *how* (that's the mission, coming up next), but the *why*. They're short – usually under 25 words – simple and inspirational. Now have a go at writing your own vision statement. Start by asking yourself these questions:

✳ What am I trying to achieve or change?

✳ How will the world look once I'm successful?

SEARCHING FOR THE GOOD IN THINGS

Christian Kroll is an environmentalist from Berlin, who also happens to be a wonderfully progressive and radical entrepreneur. Back in 2009, while travelling around the globe in an attempt to understand the social and environmental issues we're facing, he came up with the idea to create a search engine for people who want to mitigate climate change. He launched Ecosia.org as a 'green' alternative to Google, and it uses the profits generated from people using the platform to plant trees. At the time of writing, Ecosia has planted over 165 million of them. I'm a big fan and have used it for years, so I caught up with Christian to ask him how his team (now 100 strong) stays true to the company's vision, and what advice he might have for you on your journey to doing good and getting paid:

At Ecosia, the vision is 'Solve climate change and help social and environmental justice', so it's pretty clear and easy to understand. It's why we exist. But if we zoom out a little, we know that we're also here to build easy solutions for our users so they can have a positive impact on the climate while they're browsing; that we want to scale our userbase so we have an even bigger impact on the planet; and that we can be a role model as a regenerative company. To keep the team connected to this vision, Ecosia has a meeting every Friday, and the focus is very much on impact: how many trees we've planted this week, stories from the tree-planting programmes around the world. And we prioritize celebrating the right metrics to keep us aligned – for example, we had a '100 million trees planted' party, not a $20 million revenue party. We know the money is what enables us to do the work we do, but it's not the main reason we're here. Our quarterly planning sessions are a chance for

... make sure your passion is authentic. You'll be tested ...

us to revisit the mission and guide our strategic decisions, so the mission is felt throughout the organization. Ultimately it's why people have chosen to work for us. Our team is intrinsically motivated by our impact, so the key for us is aligning with their motivation and what they want to create in the world.

The other aspect to our vision, being a role model to other start-ups and companies, is also a big part of what we do. I was very reluctant at the beginning to allow any investment in Ecosia, because I didn't want to change the purpose of the company to become focused on delivering a greater financial return. So it took a long time to grow, as we were self-financing the organization. But back in 2019 we made a legally binding commitment that Ecosia can never be sold, and it's impossible to take profits out of the company. So we're basically a not-for-profit company but still a business, which means we can make as much money as we like and reinvest it in the business, but that it's impossible for any other organization to take control over it. Even if Microsoft or Google came along with a billion-dollar cheque now, it would be impossible to sell. I could have earned a lot of money, but my co-owner, Tim Schumacher, and I decided not to do that. Instead we gave 99.9 per cent of our shares away to the foundation and just kept the voting rights, so that we can still run it as a normal business – it just means there are no dividends and no potential exit. That was the important part for us, because ultimately, we're growing a movement not a business.

Other than baking in your mission to your operations and structure, my three pieces of advice to anyone starting out on this journey would be as follows. Get a great mentor; if your founding team doesn't have somebody with heaps of experience, you definitely need to source it from outside. Next, make sure you have a good business model and be realistic, because you don't want to be reliant on handouts or goodwill. Finally, make sure your passion is authentic. You'll be tested in the early years as you build your mission and team, but if you're genuinely passionate about your cause you'll find the energy to keep going.

TWITTER: @CHRISTIAN_KROLL/@ECOSIA

Check out purpose-economy.org for more inspiration and information about how organizations such as Ecosia are re-envisioning the nature of corporate ownership.

Mission

If the vision is your guiding star – how the world will look when you're done – your mission is how you're going to make it happen. Ultimately you want your mission to be crystal clear and to define the line of business you're in, why your company or campaign exists, and who it's serving. It can also be where you define your values, ethics, culture and goals – so that your stakeholders (staff, volunteers, audience, funders, partners and so on) instantly 'get' what you're about. Here's City to Sea's: *'Our mission is to prevent plastic pollution at source by awakening active hope, championing practical solutions and inspiring positive action that serves to protect and restore wildlife, rivers and seas.'*

Here are some examples of world-leading, purpose-led missions around the globe to get your creative juices flowing.

Tesla, an American electric vehicle and clean energy company. Like it or loathe it, it has a brilliant mission statement.
To accelerate the world's transition to sustainable energy.

Watts of Love, a US-based NGO providing solar technology and education to those living in poverty.
Watts of Love is a global solar lighting non-profit bringing people the power to raise themselves out of the darkness of poverty.

Chilly's, creators of reusable products such as bottles, coffee cups and food pots.
Accelerate the adoption and everyday use of reusable products.

Ecover, the world's largest producer of ecological detergents and eco-friendly cleaning and laundry products.
We're on a mission to lead a clean world revolution.

If you're feeling ready to have a crack at your mission – even just a draft one at this stage – start by asking yourself *what* you're doing, *how* you're doing it and *who* it benefits. Ideally, it'll be one snappy sentence, or a paragraph at the most.

If you're planning on applying for funding for your project, if it's a charity or non-profit, you might also want to build out your mission into your Theory of Change (ToC). A ToC is a deep dive into your aims and plans, a reason to discuss them with others and to clarify and articulate them, and it's worth putting in the time to develop this early on. It is key for funders, because it enables them to understand clearly how you'll make a difference. It links your activities to outcomes (your impact) and shows how their support can help you achieve your overall goals in the short, medium and long term. Helpfully, it can be represented in a visual diagram, as a narrative, or both.

... start by asking yourself what you're doing, how you're doing it and who it benefits.

Your ToC also gives you a clear and testable theory about how change will happen, which in turn gives you a robust framework for monitoring and evaluation (more on that later).

To create it, go through the following process, ideally working with members of your team or co-creators:

1. Outline the problem: clarify the problem you're addressing and its underlying cause.

2. Agree your aims: outline your long-term and specific aims.

3. Map outcomes: work backwards to figure out what needs to happen to achieve your aims.

4. Identify activities and outputs: state what you are going to do.

5. Specify indicators and targets: explain what you will use to assess your progress and success.

6. Test the theory and adjust: this is a living document that you evolve as you go.

There are entire books and workshops on developing your ToC, and for good reason – it takes time and skill to create a really good one. But if time and skill are in short supply, you might like to take the '10 Minute Theory of Change Challenge' developed by Sally Cupitt, head of NCVO Charities Evaluation Services (ncvo.org.uk). She believes you can tell your story in the style of an 'elevator pitch', in three sentences of no more than 20 words each. This is effectively a very simple form of theory of change, articulating what you do, the immediate changes you bring about, and the longer-term change you contribute to.

Here's her ToC example, based on the brilliant work done by NCVO Charities Evaluation Services:

1. NCVO Charities Evaluation Services offers consultancy, training and resources to the voluntary sector and its funders.

2. This increases knowledge and skills in evaluation, which helps people collect better data to inform their decision-making.

3. This, in turn, helps organizations improve their services, which helps improve the lives of vulnerable people at the frontline.

Sounds clear, doesn't it? Here are Sally's tips for creating your own ten-minute ToC:

1. Statement one describes what you do and who you work with. It effectively describes your outputs and target group.

2. Statement two describes the changes you hope to make in your client group. These are your outcomes. This and statement three talk only about changes in your user group (or whatever the target of your work is); neither statement should contain information about you or your services. Of course, in a full theory of change there may be layers of outcomes that happen at different times.

3. Statement three talks about your impact. This should talk about broader, longer-term changes, often beyond your client group. This statement is similar to a mission statement in many charities.

So start with a ten-minute ToC and see how you get on. If you're planning on building a campaigning organization, or going for some serious grant or philanthropic funding, it's worth checking out more of the ToC resources on the NCVO website. For now, though, if you've worked through those questions, you should be clear about what you are going to do, why you are going to do it, and how.

Values

You've got your vision and your mission aligned and drafted, so you have a general sense of where you're heading, why you're heading there and how you're going to get there. (They can be on the back of an envelope at this stage, or in note form on your phone. You're not running a massive operation – yet – so it doesn't need to be too polished.) Next, we're going to put some solid foundations under your dreams in the shape of your mission's *values*.

Your values are essentially the guiding principles of how you – or your company, project or campaign – behave and act, and what you stand for. They help everyone involved in your mission to stay aligned and work towards a common goal, as well as helping with communication, decision-making and partnerships. Basically, if it doesn't align with your values, you can let it go.

An example of a company that walks its talk, literally, is Vivobarefoot. Founded in 2012 by two seventh-generation cobblers, Galahad and Asher Clark (you may recognize the Clarks shoes connection), the whole company, from product (ethical, regenerative footwear) to people (how they show up in the world as a brand), is an embodiment of their values. Theirs are:

DANCE: Move More.
Continuous improvement, constant collaboration.
Small steps, relax.

SIMPLICITY: Walk the Talk.
Honesty, focus, celebrate failure quickly.

DIVERSITY: Be an Outsider.
Step outside your comfort zone, be creative, innovative and regenerative.

Through living their values, internally and externally, they've managed to create a successful shoe company and community that does good, from foot health to planetary health.

At City to Sea, we spent a lot of time defining and refining our values, and we embed them in our work from board to beach. We use them to set the tone of our communications (on social media, for example), to evaluate potential partnerships and to develop as individuals. Ours are:

EARTH KIND. We don't just appreciate nature, we love it. Nature is our best buddy, our trusted advisor and our most important board member.

POSITIVE. We praise progress and listen to all perspectives, while remaining authentic. We believe a tickle is better than a punch, and keep our messaging upbeat and playful.

BRAVE. We take risks with our content and embrace our mistakes. We dream big and make magic happen.

CREATIVE. We keep our messaging simple when facing complex issues. We improvise, imagine and inspire, embracing diversity and seeking inclusion.

BALANCED. We're a critical friend and trusted peer. In a world of fake news and greenwashing, we take time to find out the facts and evaluate our impact.

Our values don't just sit in a document somewhere or on the website doing nothing; they're a code, a way of life that informs our campaigns, our content, even our personal development plans and competencies. Have a go yourself now by circling four or five ideas from the list opposite, or come up with your own that are meaningful for you and your mission. As you're doing this, imagine you're laying the foundations, or a shared 'code of conduct', for the community you'll be creating. This shared ethos will form the framework for how you grow. If you don't intentionally own, care about and model the values, things may get blurry or confusing down the line. Stick your chosen words somewhere you'll keep seeing them for a couple of weeks. After a month, decide whether they still feel good, or if some aren't quite right. Keep them fresh, alive and meaningful and you'll notice them rippling out, almost effortlessly, through your work.

ACCOUNTABLE	EMPATHETIC
ADAPTABLE	EMPOWERING
ADVENTUROUS	ENERGETIC
AGILE	EQUITABLE
ALTRUISTIC	FEARLESS
AWARE	FIERCE
BALANCED	FLUID
BOLD	FRESH
BRAVE	GENEROUS
CARING	GIVING
CHALLENGING	GLOBAL
CHEERFUL	GRATEFUL
COLLABORATIVE	HARMONIOUS
COMPASSIONATE	HELPFUL
CONSCIOUS	HONEST
DEDICATED	IMAGINATIVE
DEMOCRATIC	INNOVATIVE
DIFFERENT	INTERSECTIONAL
DIVERSE	JOYFUL

LEADING	RESPECTFUL
LOGICAL	SENSITIVE
LOVING	SILLY
MAGICAL	SIMPLE
MEANINGFUL	SPIRITED
MINDFUL	STRUCTURED
NIMBLE	SUSTAINABLE
OPEN-MINDED	TIMELY
OPTIMISTIC	TOLERANT
ORIGINAL	TRANSPARENT
OUTRAGEOUS	TRUSTING
PASSIONATE	UNIQUE
PEACEFUL	UNITED
PERSISTENT	USEFUL
PLAYFUL	VALUABLE
POSITIVE	VISIONARY
REGENERATIVE	WELCOMING
RELIABLE	WILD
RESOURCEFUL	WISE
	WONDER

Intersectionality

Vision, mission, values … and beyond. From the start, make sure you've mapped the other issues, injustices or forms of exclusion that intersect with your mission, and where your mission overlaps with others.

The American lawyer and civil rights advocate Kimberlé Crenshaw developed the theory of intersectionality in 1989. She opened up the conversation around what happens when two or more forms of exclusion overlap, suggesting that at the point where they intersect, that person or group is likely to experience double the harm. For example, as a woman, I've experienced discrimination, but as a white, able-bodied, cisgender person, there's a whole load of oppression I have the privilege of not experiencing. People whose identities overlap various minority groups, whether of sexual orientation, gender, race or body type, are more likely to experience more than one form of discrimination and inequality.

Vision, mission, values … and beyond.

Looking at this through the lens of environmentalism, and as highlighted and championed by the US-based environmentalist Leah Thomas (@greengirlleah), the effects of ecosystem collapse – changing climate, pollution and pandemics – are felt disproportionately by those with less privilege. Globally it's women, marginalized communities and Black, Indigenous and People of Colour (BIPOC) communities who are affected most by environmental issues, from rural farmers losing their water supplies to city-dwellers feeling the effects of air pollution. Yet all too often (hands up – I've been part of this in the past), well-meaning environmentalists have failed to acknowledge and dismantle the structural and systemic racism that means marginalized communities are hardest hit.

Let's apply this to the problem of plastic. When you think of plastic pollution, you might think of a whale with plastic in its stomach, or a turtle with a straw up its nose, or even Sir David Attenborough's programme *Blue Planet*. Maybe you visualize surfers doing beach cleans, or trendy local zero-waste shops. But if we zoom out and look again through an inter-sectional lens, we see a lot more. We see the people living closest to the fracking sites and refineries, known as 'fence line communities', who are typically BIPOC communities, suffering health problems caused by the toxic extraction and production processes of the plastic industry. A live example of this at the time of writing is Formosa Plastics, which is constructing a new facility in St James Parish, Louisiana, where 87 per cent of the residents are Black. (Check out @peakplastic on Instagram if you want to learn more.)

At the other end of plastic's polluting life cycle, if it doesn't make its way into the ocean, it may end up in landfill or be incinerated, again affecting the marginalized, low-income communities closest to the toxic, leaching landfill sites or air-polluting incinerators. Even when we think we've done the right thing by recycling, we find our plastic's been exported to countries in the majority world where waste-pickers, who are mostly women, face dangerous conditions and health risks picking through our contaminated trash. To tell the story of plastic pollution only through pictures of beach litter and dead marine animals is to ignore the impact of environmental racism. For real, lasting change to happen, we must include everyone.

So, whether you're campaigning for animal rights, trying to stop mobile-phone masts from being erected next to your local school, or focusing on a global problem like biodiversity loss, make sure you've understood who's affected and centre their voices and stories alongside, or even above, your own.

INTERSECTIONAL FROM THE HEART, INTERSECTIONAL FROM THE START

Kumi Naidoo is a social and environmental activist with 40 years' experience of changing the world for the better. He was international executive director of Greenpeace International and secretary general of Amnesty International, and is a tireless and passionate advocate for human rights. I asked him what people who are looking to get into activism, or start their own non-profit or business, should be thinking about:

After four decades in the field, I can tell you that activism is seriously broken. The large organizations that have been around for decades are failing us … otherwise why are we still in such deep shit? Albert Einstein said, 'the definition of insanity is doing the same thing over and over again and expecting to get different results.' If I'm brutally honest, my life ticks off that definition of insanity, which is why I'm focusing on what we need to do differently now. We have to look at the old problems that my generation was not able to resolve, and bring fresh solutions … and we need a deep understanding of intersectionality.

One of the things the feminist movement gave us decades ago – the biggest gift that activism could have ever received, which was largely scoffed at by mainstream activism – was the word 'intersectionality'. The power in that word, the conceptual power, is fundamental for this moment and one of the main reasons we're failing to address the many issues that we're facing on Planet Earth. We're stuck in a very siloed way of operating – focused on human rights, or the environment, or poverty inequality or gender – without understanding how these things are fundamentally connected. This is why I believe the most effective activists and changemakers of the future will be those who have genuinely adopted an intersectional approach.

I believe the most effective activists and changemakers of the future will be those who have genuinely adopted an intersectional approach.

So how to do this when you're starting out? First and foremost, respond to your heart. Respond to that which makes you want to cry, want to do something about it. Respond to what makes you think, 'I'll never be a full human being until I've done something to address that.' Whatever the issue is, no matter how uninteresting or sexy it is in other people's eyes, just follow it. But once you make the decision to act, ask yourself, 'How does this relate to all the other things that are happening around me?' I recommend doing a matrix or a simple drawing, and putting your issue at the centre. Then look at how your issue relates to education, how it relates to the environ-

ment, transport, the economy, inequality etc. You don't have to create a perfect map of every intersection there is; choose the five or six things you feel are most relevant to your mission and resonate with your values.

We've got a very, very tiny window of opportunity that is fast closing to make the changes we need to see in the world. So if you want to be a twenty-first-century activist and live in the moment, choose whichever thing speaks to your heart the most [and] do it in an intersectional way. Watch videos on it, read books, and be willing to look at your own practices and do things differently.

INSTAGRAM: @KUMINAIDOO

To listen to the full interview on intersectionality, decentralized organizing and stories from Kumi's extraordinary life, go to nataliefee.com/dogoodgetpaid.

Structure

If you're planning on volunteering for the entire length of your campaign or project and you don't need to raise any money to make it happen, you can probably do it without a formal legal structure. But this is a book about doing good and getting paid, so I assume there will be financial transactions. In that case, you need to decide what structure suits you and your mission.

Ideally, you've got an idea for doing good that's not going to depend on trusts, grants and foundations. In other words, you've got a service to offer that solves a social and/or environmental problem and has a commercial element. With around 1.7 million active non-profit organizations registered in the

USA, over 160,000 registered charities in England and Wales, and around 60,000 charitable organizations in Australia, competition for grant funding is tough, so the sooner you come up with a business model for your mission, the better. That said, 70–80 per cent of charities in the UK earn the majority of their income from contracts rather than grants or donations, so it's worth exploring the pros and cons of the different legal structures that are available.

Freelancers and sole traders/proprietors

If it's just you and maybe a couple of others working with you, and you're going to be paid for delivering a service to clients rather than applying for grant funding, you can be a freelancer. The official structure for this in the UK and USA is a sole trader or proprietor, which means you run your own business and you're registered as self-employed. This is a quick and easy way to start working for yourself, as a freelancer or consultant, getting paid for your time and skills by the hour or the day. You'll need to register with Her Majesty's Revenue and Customs (HMRC) in the UK, or the Small Business Development Center (SBDC) in the USA, and then you're off, ready to earn money doing what you love. This does mean you're personally liable for the debts of the business, and you'll need to do your accounts or hire an accountant to submit your annual taxes.

'FUCKING SHIT UP AND DOING THINGS DIFFERENTLY': FROM VOLUNTEER TO INVESTOR IN FIVE YEARS

Sabia Wade, the Black Doula, is a visionary, super-savvy 33-year-old educator and entrepreneur based in the USA. Her radical approach to reproductive justice and her focus on elevating the voices and experiences of marginalized communities have seen her transition from a 'broke as fuck' volunteer with the Prison Birth Project in 2015 to CEO of her own company with a $650,000 turnover and founder of the non-profit For the Village – a community doula programme that provides free and low-cost doula services to under-represented communities – within five years.

Having experienced the complexities that came with being Black and queer in a corporate environment in her early twenties, Sabia knew she wanted to do things differently. She wanted to work in medicine, but in a way that allowed her to do things her way, for the people she felt needed her the most, and so she decided to train as a doula. After two years as a volunteer, learning about birth, obstetric violence, the Black maternal crisis and reproductive justice, Sabia set up her own doula practice in San Diego.

Generally, over the past six years, when she's had an opportunity to do something unconventional, she's done it. When she was advised not to focus her business on marginalized people, because they'd typically be from a lower socio-economic background and wouldn't be able to afford her services, she proved them wrong; within a year she was charging $2,000 per client and experiencing unprecedented demand. But although this new-found abundance was meeting her need to earn a living, it wasn't meeting her desire to scale and to serve the wider community.

In order to offer free doula services to under-represented communities, in 2018 Sabia set up For The Village, Inc., a not-for-profit focusing on marginalized groups, such as People of Colour, LGBTQ+ and low-income families, and also on improving Black maternal health outcomes through doula support and education. It focuses on marginalized groups, such as people of colour, LGBTQ+ and low-income families, and also on improving Black maternal health outcomes through doula support and education. It attracts a stable stream of grants of around $50,000 a year, and at the time of writing, Sabia had just heard that For the Village had been awarded $100,000 as a donation from Blue Cross Blue Shield, a US-based health association. The following year, as For The Village was growing, Sabia also decided to create Birthing Advocacy Doula Trainings (BADT), to train birth workers seeking to go beyond the standard doula role and into advocacy for the under-represented. It's been an incredible success. In 2019, their first year, BADT generated $25,000. In 2020, the income of BADT, together with Sabia's brand, The Black Doula, had quadrupled to $100,000. In 2021 BADT launched in Canada, and together with TBD, made just about $650,000. They are on track to make even more in 2022.

Don't be afraid to create your own table, don't be afraid to stand out and be yourself

Sabia puts her success down to creating opportunity, not just for herself but also for people in her community, and to her *commitment to showing others who face similar structural and systemic barriers that it is possible to generate wealth doing something you believe in. Her advice for you? 'Don't be afraid to create your own table, don't be afraid to stand out and be yourself. By putting your idea or project out there, by creating your own space, your own table or your own organization, you'll fill a space that maybe you needed for yourself, but then people start coming who were looking for it too. It's beautiful. And then it just grows and before you know it you have a business that's bigger than you.'*

INSTAGRAM: @THEBLACKDOULA

Social enterprise

Generally, the term 'social enterprise' is used to describe a business that exists to achieve a social or environmental mission; it's not a legal structure in itself. There are lots of structures to choose from if you're setting up a social venture, but if you're planning on a mix of income streams, including grants and donations, choose your legal structure carefully. According to UnLtd, a UK-based charity set up to find, fund and support social entrepreneurs, the most common legal structures used in the social entrepreneurship sector are:

✳ Unincorporated association (which could also be a registered charity)

✳ Company limited by guarantee (which could also be a registered charity)

✳ Company limited by shares (which could also be a B Corp; see below)

✳ Community Benefit Society or Cooperative Societies (previously known as Industrial & Provident Society) – *UK only*

✳ Community interest company or CIC (shares or guarantee) – *UK only*

B KIND, B CORP

If you want to go down the for-profit route and have a limited company with, conversely, no limits when it comes to making a profit, you might want to become a B Corp (or B Corporation). These are privately certified companies that are legally required to consider the impact of their decisions on their workers, customers, suppliers, community and the environment.

B Corps have to be totally transparent about their operational activities, and must be recertified every two years. If you fail to meet the set criteria, you'll lose your B Corp status. It's pretty robust and reliable in terms of certification, but it takes time and good governance to keep up. What's extra-cool about B Corp certification is that the criteria aren't set in stone, so each year the standards are updated to make sure B Corps are in line with the latest science and information about social and environmental justice.

It's not easy to become a B Corp, which is a good thing, because it means it's not greenwashing and only businesses that are serious about their ethics pass the test. You'll need to complete (and get a good score in) the B Impact Assessment and sign the rather fantastic declaration of interdependence:

We envision a global economy that uses business as a force for good.

This economy is comprised of a new type of corporation – the B Corporation – which is purpose-driven and creates benefit for all stakeholders, not just shareholders.

As B Corporations and leaders of this emerging economy, we believe:

— *That we must be the change we seek in the world.*

— *That all business ought to be conducted as if people and place mattered.*

— *That, through their products, practices and profits, businesses should aspire to do no harm and benefit all.*

— *To do so requires that we act with the understanding that we are each dependent upon another and thus responsible for each other and future generations.*

Being a certified B Corp is a brilliant way of stating your intention to do good in the world, while doing no harm. Being certified also connects you to a global community of B Corps and B Leaders … and from there the world's your organic, carbon-sequestering oyster.

It's not easy to become a B Corp, which is a good thing

Can I CIC it?

When it became clear that City to Sea was taking off and we were starting to build momentum, I decided to make things more official, and switch from a team of four freelancers to setting up a Community Interest Company (CIC). I sought advice before

doing so, getting free support from local voluntary organizations and helpful lawyers specializing in charity law who were
happy to have a coffee and talk through options. Being a CIC
has worked for us over the years in terms of being more agile
and less onerous in terms of governance and reporting, but
it has restricted us in terms of unlocking some larger grants
from trusts and foundations, and also means we're not eligible
for Gift Aid. As a result, some five years later, we're setting up
a charity to operate alongside our CIC. We're going to get a
bit technical now, so feel free to skip this section if you know
a CIC isn't for you.

CICs were set up by the UK government in 2005 and are
designed to work as businesses that use their profits for public
good rather than for shareholders and owners. The aim is
for them to help create a sustainable and socially inclusive
economy, although they can't be politically motivated. A CIC
can be a Company Limited by Shares (CLS; in which case you
have a dividend cap, meaning shareholders can't receive more
than 35 per cent of the company's
profits in dividends) or a Company
Limited by Guarantee (CLG, a
company that has no share capital
and cannot pay dividends).

*A charity
must have a
clear charita-
ble purpose*

A CIC is designed to be more
flexible than a charity, and it's
relatively straightforward to get
started. You can do the initial set-up online via Companies
House, and it costs just £27. Probably because of this, CICs
are incredibly popular in the UK; by 2020, just under 19,000
had been registered.

The downside is that a CIC will not have the same tax advantages as a charity; CICs are liable for corporation tax in the same way as any other limited company. Each year a CIC must submit information to Companies House with evidence of social impact or benefit for that financial year. Overall, a CIC is a great option for a new social enterprise, but do your research and ensure that you choose the structure best suited to your objectives, stakeholders and business model.

Setting up a charity

Before setting up as a charity or non-profit, it's worth checking that there isn't already a brilliant one out there doing what you'd like yours to do. If there really isn't, or if any existing ones don't want to collaborate, take time to consider whether you even want to run an organization that for the most part will have to remain dependent on grants and the generosity of others.

A charity must have a clear charitable purpose, so do your research to check yours is recognized as a priority by funders. It's not particularly difficult to set up a charity, but it's not so easy to find the funding to keep it going and create lasting change.

Charitable structures have more tax advantages than other legal structures, but are more heavily regulated. Also, members of the board of a charity can be paid only if it is considered to be in the best interests of the charity and if the constitution contains that power. Therefore, the founder is usually controlled by a board of volunteers or trustees.

The most common structure in the USA is charitable organizations that fall into the category of Section 501(c)(3) of the IRS rules, so that's the one to check out first. (If you want to geek out on the other 26 types of structure, head to upcounsel.com/types-of-nonprofits.) In Australia, the Australian Charities and Not-for-profits Commission has loads of helpful advice on its website, acnc.gov.au. In the UK there are four main types of charity structure to explore:

Charitable Incorporated Organization (CIO)

These are a newer offering for people wanting to set up a charity in the UK, having been around since 2013. They're more lightweight than a charitable company, allowing you to incorporate and get the benefits available to conventional charities without the burden of being regulated by both the Charity Commission and Companies House. The only downside is that a CIO can't get a mortgage (say you wanted to buy an office instead of renting one), so the Charity Commission suggests that the CIO structure will probably suit only smaller to medium-sized charities, those without significant assets.

Charitable Company (limited by guarantee)

This is the most common structure, in which the activities of the charity are governed by the articles of association, which are registered at Companies House. To be called 'charitable', you have to demonstrate, through your governing document (Memorandum and Articles of Association), that you have solid charitable aims and that your work is for public or planetary benefit. Unlike the CIO structure, a Charitable Company has its own legal personality (sadly it's not *that* fun) and can enter into contracts with other organizations and hold property in its own name. The downside? You'll need to submit two filings, to Companies House and to the Charity Commission.

Unincorporated Association

This is a form of charity suitable for community groups or volunteers with a shared mission. You'll need to draw up and agree a constitution to help your group run smoothly, and, as with other charity structures, that must include aims (or objects) that are exclusively charitable. You'll be able to apply for grants that are available only to charities, but the big downside is that you won't be able to employ staff or own premises.

Charitable Trust

This structure is usually suitable for a group of people ('trustees') who want to manage assets such as money, investments, land or buildings. Unlike other charitable structures, charitable trusts are set up not to fulfil a purpose or mission, but to distribute funds that help others fulfil their purpose. So this is more suitable for philanthropists, family trusts and foundations.

ZAYTOUN: A STORY FROM THE OLIVE GROVES OF PALESTINE

In 2004 an idea was born under the heavy shadow of Israeli restrictions on Palestinians' rights to travel, trade and access their land. Atif Choudhury, a young neurodiverse Bangladeshi who had left school at 16, had been volunteering in Palestine with the International Solidarity Movement. But he wanted to do more to support the farmers there, to go beyond aid and help to re-establish a sustainable livelihood for olive-growers and their families. So that year he co-founded Zaytoun and pledged to reinvest 100 per cent of its profits into this mission.

Faced with a lot of risk, they decided to 'crowdsource' pre-orders, way before this existed as a mainstream method, by using Yahoo Groups. Atif asked people to pledge money to support Palestinian livelihoods, and hundreds did, giving him hope that there might be a business opportunity. Zaytoun raised £36,000 ($66,500) from this grassroots funding, allowing it to move a container of olive oil from Palestinian farmers to the UK. This process was carried out in close collaboration with communities in Palestine, leveraging their understanding of domestic challenges, a practice that Zaytoun has continued to the present day.

Yet even with this swell of support, funding and collaboration didn't make imports easy. Palestine's only port, in Gaza, was placed under a ten-year embargo and so the trucks of oil had to go through the West Bank. Eventually, the first full shipment of Palestinian olive oil arrived in the UK, but when Atif opened it, he found that, disastrously, most of the bottles had been smashed. Not one to wallow in his setbacks (or in gallons of olive oil), he set about borrowing money from Triodos Bank, one of the most sustainable banks operating in the UK. Combined with growing support, including from politicians such as the UK Green Party's Caroline Lucas, Zaytoun kept going. However, when the second container was misdirected to Italy and took four months to trace, Atif began to doubt whether Zaytoun's mission was even possible. He felt that 'smarter people will come along to make this work and they can learn from our mistakes, but it's not going to be us.' Happily, he was wrong.

Zaytoun's team, then four, maximized media attention, diversified their imports by purchasing tracked containers, and continued to listen to the advice of Palestinian families. This last tactic inspired the company to offer a wider variety of products, such as za'atar. Despite initial disbelief from the Fairtrade Foundation, Zaytoun succeeded in making the world's first Fairtrade olive oil in 2009.

Zaytoun has managed to thrive, growing from 22 farmers in a single village to working with a network of 6,000 families in 26 villages

With these shifts, and growing success, Atif decided to change Zaytoun's business model from a limited company to a CIC. These hadn't existed when Zaytoun was founded; it was only the second company in the UK to use this new model. It was a way to signal the benefit the brand was having. It also avoided the lengthier process of registering as a charity and being restricted by the Charity Commission, which Atif perceives as being influenced by UK foreign policy in a way that might limit Zaytoun's ability to comment freely on the situation in Palestine.

When asked about Zaytoun's success today, and whether his thoughts on profit have changed, Atif maintains his stance of 'purpose beyond profit'. He believes that organizations should make a profit, because this reduces dependency on grants that 'may make or break what social good you get to do'. For Atif, a *sustainable profit is necessary, and the real question is what a company does with this profit.*

Atif's journey with Zaytoun has been challenging, rewarding and constantly dynamic. Some struggles have persisted; the supply chain from Palestine to the UK is as difficult as ever, with Palestine remaining a captured economy. But throughout, Zaytoun has managed to thrive, growing from 22 farmers in a single village to working with a network of 6,000 families in 26 villages, all able to trade with the UK, something that was once thought impossible. In terms of the products, things have never tasted so good, and Zaytoun's olive oil was crowned the Nation's Favourite organic product in a publicly voted category at the annual organic industry awards in 2021. Atif reflects on his career with Zaytoun as difficult, but says reassuringly that 'all good ideas are; they should frighten us.'

RESOURCES

* UnLtd: www.unltd.org.uk
* The School for Social Entrepreneurs: www.the-sse.org
* The National Council for Voluntary Organisations: www.ncvo.org.uk

Money

Right, let's get down to the nitty-gritty. If you're looking at building something that can grow, scale up and sustain you and your team, you need a good business idea that will generate a steady income. Having a robust business model that you can test out and refine means you won't be reliant on donations, grants or goodwill from others. It's the one thing we didn't do early on at City to Sea. Grant funders are increasingly keen to fund organizations that won't remain dependent on grants, so look at this from the start, whether you're planning on being a charity or a social enterprise. Libraries of books and hundreds of videos are available on developing your business model, so I won't go into that here, but you could start by looking up 'business model canvas' and running through it a few times to get into the right mindset. Essentially, if you can come up with a product or service that the world needs, you can generate a steady income that, if you do it right, will give you a degree of financial security. Most charities have a trading arm – basically a separate business owned by the charity – that generates funding for their charitable work, so whatever your structure, if you're in it for the long run, get your business model nailed first.

If you're a non-profit, you can diversify your income streams and get all kinds of funding in addition to your business revenue, generating money from your business while simultaneously unlocking grants, donations and even investment. Let's look at that part now.

Show. Me. The. Money.

Securing funding for your project, product or people is essential in helping you decide what you can achieve, so you must get comfortable with making money and asking for financial help, or, at least, get confident going outside your comfort zone, for the sake of your mission. People can become really awkward and challenged by the idea of asking for help, especially when there's money involved. So, here's the first thing to remember:

You're not asking people for money for you personally; you're asking on behalf of your cause.

This is key in terms of getting comfortable with asking for money. It's not about you. You're the personality, the salesperson, the organizer; you need to convince your audience – whether that's a grant funder, a philanthropist or your family and friends – that your cause is worth giving to. You're the vehicle through which this amazing work is going to happen. And yes, you will be paid fairly to do the work. But it's not personal. Once you really get that, once you're really connected to the outcome and what the funding will enable, asking for financial help becomes an adventure.

you must get comfortable making money and asking for financial help

You'll also need to be cool with a 'no'. There'll be a lot of those, so prepare yourself for people not getting why this is so important, not having the resources to help you, or just being too busy to give it any thought. A 'no' can be painful, especially when you've spent weeks on a grant application and months in talks with funders to get a donation over the line. But you'll get better at picking yourself up, dusting yourself off and making the next ask, and the next one. Again, it's not personal, even though it might feel it, and there are plenty of people and organizations out there who will understand and will want to support you financially. Just keep asking and being creative about the value – either material or immaterial – your donors get in return for their help.

Budgets make cents

Next, you need to know roughly how much to ask for. This may be obvious to some, but the cost of a campaign or new venture varies wildly depending on scale and existing resources. When it comes to doing good and getting paid, budgets can be broken down into two categories:

Organizational budget
These usually run for a year (ideally matching your financial year) and cover your overall operations, from staff costs to overheads (office costs, stationery, internet and so on). In funding terms, especially for non-profits, these are known as core costs.

Campaign budget
This is a specific breakdown of the costs incurred from a particular action, campaign or project. If you're not setting up a company, you can include your (and others') freelance rate in this. Depending on the campaign, the budget might include filmmaking costs, social media advertising, graphic and website design, art supplies and so on.

A quick search for 'non-profit organizational budget' or 'charity campaign budget' will set you off in the right direction if you don't know where to begin.

Diversifying your funding streams

As well as having a handle on your figures, it's also a good idea to have a range of different income sources, so you're not too dependent on one. Here are a few options:

Grants, trusts and foundations
Grants can be an excellent way to help you get established and trial new initiatives, because they provide money that doesn't need to be paid back. Whoop! Free money! They're offered by a range of philanthropic, government and charitable bodies, which are effectively investing in the social or environmental outcomes and impacts that you provide. But – and it's a big but – they're not easy to come by. When you're starting out, you don't have a track record, so it can be hard to convince funders that you're trustworthy and that your project is actually going to make a difference. (If you've created your Theory of Change, see page 95, this is exactly where you're going to need it.)

Grant-writing is a world unto itself, so to write your applications you'll need either someone who's good with words and communicating social and environmental impact, or someone who's got fundraising experience. If you don't have the means to pay, you could put a shout out for pro bono grant-writers or ex-grant-writers willing to look over your applications and give you feedback before you send them. They may even help you write them.

There are some notable grant-funding bodies, among them the Arts Council, Big Lottery and UnLtd, but there are also hundreds of smaller funders of different types. Consider registering with one of the many excellent platforms, such as

My Funding Central and Grants Online (UK) or Foundation Directory Online and GrantScape (USA), where you can search for funding based on specific criteria such as your size, your location, who you work with and the impact you want to have. You can register for regular e-updates, too, so that you get alerts as new funds open. It's important to check these frequently; some have really short application windows, so you don't want to miss out. Try registering with your local council and community/voluntary sector umbrella support bodies (search online for 'voluntary sector support [your town/city]'), which can be great sources of advice and information, and local government may have grants for small businesses or social enterprises too.

What's the kindest, most creative way of getting their attention?

The downside of sourcing money through grants, trusts and foundations is that it takes a lot of time, energy and resources, and your chances of success are relatively low. That's not to say it's not worth it – it absolutely is – but it's best if grants are just one of your revenue or income streams.

Partnerships/CSR

As I explained above, partnerships have been City to Sea's funding sweet spot. This may be because of my background in business (if we can call it that), or because it's generally more fun and engaging than grant funding. Partnerships with like-minded organizations can be a win-win, helping corporates or smaller businesses achieve their Corporate and Social Responsibility (CSR) goals or reach new audiences, while helping to power your mission financially. Effective partnerships can be creative, dynamic and impactful. Obviously, you must be aware of greenwashing – corporations that want to look as though they're doing the right thing while still engaging in major social or environmental injustices – so make sure you scrutinize their policies and do some ethical screening. We love using Ethical Consumer's 'Ethiscore' rating system for this.

Draw up a list of your dream partners, and alongside each write a few lines explaining why your two missions are a fit. Why would someone with a busy, demanding job as a CSR or sustainability manager for a large corporate choose to partner with you and support your mission instead of that of any other of the hundreds in their inbox? What's the kindest, most creative way of getting their attention? Then just do it. Get ready to be rejected, and get asking. At some point, you'll get a yes – usually to a phone or video call – to talk it through. Remember to do lots of research first. What are the company's goals? What communication style do they have? What's their track record on social and environmental issues? How might you be able to improve their brand awareness or CSR credentials? Do all this before jumping on a call with them, so you're prepared to convince them of the value of working together. If the call goes well, follow up with a proposal. This usually consists of a summary of your work and mission, what you want the funding for, what you'll achieve with it, how you'll report back, and what benefits they might get from supporting you.

Partnerships don't have to stop at corporates; they can be with other NGOs or community groups too. For bigger impact and to maximize your chances of success, it's vital to work with organizations with which you share a goal, or where there's a compelling narrative to explain why you're choosing to complement each other's work. This enables you to effect change more quickly and effectively, and also helps you to unlock funding and resources that might not otherwise be available to you, for example through joint funding bids, subcontracting and securing corporate partners. As with any successful relationship, openness, trust and honesty, agreed shared goals and values, and regular communication are key. Be open to saying no from time to time; if the deliverables are too much of a stretch, or the partner's expectations will put more strain on the organization, it's not worth it.

Crowdfunding
In a nutshell, this involves lots of people giving you relatively small amounts of money, instead of lots of money coming from a few individuals. (That's good too, and we'll touch on it in the Donations section on page 130.) There are three main kinds:

Rewards This is the most common type of crowdfunding for one-off campaigns, artistic projects, community groups and non-profits. It involves inviting people to donate to the cause in return for some kind of reward, such as a signed print, a mention at the end of a film, dinner at a local restaurant, downloads, albums or books. Bear in mind that you can't really run more than one of these every year, or every few years, so it's to be considered as *part* of your fundraising strategy.

Equity If you're starting out, or part of an existing organization doing good in the world, you can use some crowdfunding platforms to raise the capital you need to grow. Instead of just giving you money, people invest in your business in return for shares.

Debt finance or debt-based crowdfunding This is where investors provide you with funds in exchange for the right to have their money paid back with interest. Essentially, it's a way of getting a big loan from lots of individuals.

... hone your message, become good at telling your story ...

As we saw on page 42, crowdfunding was my route into fundraising for City to Sea. It's a great option if you're launching a new business or project, because you also get to make a splash (or a song and dance, in my case) publicly before you've even got going. It's also an excellent way to hone your message, become good at telling your story and develop your 'raving fans' or supportive network, many of whom will go on to advocate for you or even become your first customers.

Funders donate or invest through online platforms, which take care of the techy bit, but it's down to you to generate the rewards, do all the publicity and raise the funds. It's not for the faint-hearted and no doubt blood, sweat and tears will be required if you are to reach your target and get over the finish line.

There are many reward-based platforms, the most popular being Crowdfunder, GoFundMe and Kickstarter. Triodos Bank and Ethex are ethical investment platforms if you're looking for equity or debt-based crowdfunding.

Another way to raise a monthly income for your work as a campaigner, activist, artivist or craftivist is Patreon. This is a fantastic platform where creators like you can ask people to support their work through monthly subscriptions, instead of one-off payments. You'll need to keep them updated, motivated and engaged, but that can be a lot of fun and you can grow your community at the same time. To inspire you, the creators on Patreon include:

Bitesize Vegan 600+ patrons donating a total of $4,600 a month for content that increases the accessibility of veganism for non-vegans.

Black Queer & Intersectional Collective (BQIC) 220+ patrons donating a total of over $3,000 a month to support a world where Black queer, trans and intersex people can live safe, healthy and flourishing lives.

Talitha Brewer 30+ patrons donating a total of £760 a month for photo essays on refugees around the world.

Black Forager (Alexis Nikole) 350+ patrons donating a total of $1,500 a month for content on foraging wild food.

Areo 250+ patrons donating a total of £1,172 a month for writing on humanism, politics, culture, science and human rights.

Investment

If you're setting up a business, social enterprise or even a CIC, you might be interested in raising funds, or capital, through investment. This can be in the form of equity (shares) in your business, or as repayable finance to help you achieve your purpose. It's definitely not free money, and it does need to be paid back – normally with interest. However, if you've got a strong social or environmental mission, it's possible to get a 'blended' loan, part of which might be a grant. Many blended loans come with benefits (unlike traditional, commercial loans), such as being able to defer interest payments for at least twelve months while you find your feet.

Social investment isn't suitable for everyone, and it should be considered alongside other options. But if you're going for growth, have a proven business model and are confident that your mission is profitable, it's is a great way to get things off the ground. Check out goodfinance.org.uk (UK) or crunchbase .com (USA) for more information if you'd like to explore this route. Internationally, another fantastic initiative to check out if you identify as female or non-binary is Coralus (formally known as SheEO). It works on the basis of radical generosity, whereby people donate a certain amount each month (activators), which goes into a perpetuity fund that is loaned out to ventures looking for financial support.

Donations

This is where individuals or companies give you money to support your work. Charitable giving is a big thing; according to National Philanthropic Trust UK (which curates statistics on charitable giving and philanthropy in the UK), Londoners donate a total of about £2 billion ($2.6 billion) a year. Some three-quarters of Brits donated to charity in 2020, giving an average of £288 (£362) a year,[10] while the average American gave $608 (£480) in the same year. This should definitely be one of the options to consider when it comes to funding your project or your core costs if you're looking to build something lasting – especially if you're operating out of the USA, since Americans seem to be twice as generous as the British!

If you're a charity, donations are tax-free and benefit from tax relief (such as Gift Aid in the UK), which means people are more likely to donate larger sums of money. However, as a social enterprise you can use a platform such as Local Giving, where donations also benefit from Gift Aid. If you do a crowdfunder (see above), you could ask some of the contributors to become regular donors. Also speak to local businesses and organizations that support your work, to see if they would consider doing a Payroll Giving Scheme or in-house fundraiser.

Major donors, or philanthropists, are the holy grail of supporters and well worth cultivating.

Another good way to raise funds is through target-focused campaigns. These are when you try to raise a certain amount by a particular date. There's nothing like a clear call to action and a deadline to get people clicking the 'donate' button. If you have no idea how to set this kind of thing up, there are loads of online platforms that will host your fundraising campaign for a small fee per donation. A quick search for 'campaign fundraising platforms' will bring up plenty to research. You can also use this kind of targeted fundraising to respond to topical issues; for example, if a new report on air pollution is in the news, and your project is to reduce air pollution in your local community, you can run a powerful fundraising campaign that's timely and meaningful to your supporters.

There are also individual donors who give a lot more than the UK average of £24 ($32) a month. Major donors, or philanthropists, are the holy grail of supporters and well worth cultivating. From people who'll casually drop £500 ($650) into your bank account, to multimillionaires who can fund your entire operations for the next two years, philanthropists can be very, very helpful. The wealthier ones tend to work via foundations and family trusts, but don't rule out working with them directly. They can be hard to find and even harder to connect with, but all you need is one wealthy champion of your work to make the introductions and get you in the right place at the right time. Sometimes magic happens: you're just busy being awesome, doing your thing, and they find you. Again, there are entire books on fundraising, so if you're going to make a go of it as a major revenue stream, swot up first and get yourself off to a flying financial start.

Non-financial support
Sometimes people can't give you money but can give you their time, expertise or products. You might have heard of the Latin phrase *pro bono publico*, which means 'for the public good'. Consultants, legal experts or anyone with a particular skill might be happy to work for you pro bono, which basically means free of charge. Obviously this is really helpful if you're short

on cash to begin with. Pro bono support is a bit different from volunteering (see page 149), in that it lends itself to particular expertise, rather than suiting people who simply have time on their hands to help or want to get work experience.

A great resource for legal matters is Trustlaw™ (trust .org/trustlaw), the Thomson Reuters Foundation's global pro bono legal programme. We've used it for help with contractual agreements, and for advice when we were setting up the charitable arm of City to Sea. It connects high-impact NGOs and social enterprises working to create social and environmental change with the best law firms and corporate legal teams to provide free legal assistance. Totally amazing.

Other non-financial support could be by way of product donations. For example, if you're running a crowdfunder and need rewards for your supporters, you may be able to get these for free as an in-kind donation from a business that's aligned with your mission. Other ways you might use product donations could be as prizes for competitions, or office infrastructure such as desks or IT equipment. As a rule, product donations are easier to come by than money, because it costs the company in question less and gets their product in front of your audience. Product donations usually come out of the marketing budget, too, so they can be justified more easily than a cash donation.

PERI, PERI INTERESTING PARTNERSHIP

A brilliant example of product donations and corporate partnerships is pumping out of the Langa Township in Cape Town, South Africa. Bridges for Music was set up in 2013 by

Valentino Barrioseta, a music promoter who, after four years of running the infamously hedonistic Ibizan club, Amnesia, had become disillusioned with the industry. He'd gotten into music promoting to bring people together, to have a shared experience of something magical and transcendental, but over the years the growth of the VIP lounges, expensive bottles of champagne and chichi clientele started to wear thin. Valentino took a sabbatical to reconnect with his passion and purpose and ended up discovering a common theme on his travels. From the favelas of Brazil to the townships of South Africa he met local musicians, leaders in their towns or villages, who were also social activists making a difference, through music, in their communities.

Ultimately it's all about creating shared value in the partnership

'I remember the spark that got me thinking was this guy in Brazil, telling me how he was saving money for a new mixer so he could teach the local kids in his living room. I knew that any brand would send this guy equipment – we used to get all the latest kit for free every season in Ibiza – whereas here was this guy doing amazing things in his community but without the contacts in the right companies. So that's where the concept and name for Bridges for Music came about; I thought we could create a platform that connected stakeholders in the music industry with community projects that need their resources and could enable them to have a bigger impact.'

Fast-forward nine years and Bridges for Music has built and is currently operating a pioneering creative academy in Langa township, just a few minutes outside of Cape Town, and has another one projected in Johannesburg. The Langa campus gives 200 students a year access to world-class facilities, including recording studios and computer labs with the latest technology. It's a success story that has seen the likes of Ed Sheeran, Skrillex and Richie Hawtin supporting through workshops and raising awareness for the initiative. I asked Valentino to tell me a bit about their corporate partnerships, as it seems to be one of Bridges for Music's superpowers.

'It didn't come easy, but it's absolutely been worth the effort. Take Pioneer DJ for example. At first, support came through my old friends in the company who believed in the vision ... they'd send us free kit which we could distribute to the people who needed it most. Then, over the years, we proved ourselves and slowly managed to get buy-in from higher up in the organization, until recently we secured a yearly CSR commitment – something that's game-changing for our operations.

'Ultimately it's all about creating shared value in the partnership: if it makes business sense for them as well as meeting their social or environmental criteria, you've got a chance for a long-term partnership. With Nandos, for example, as they're interested in nurturing Africa's creativity and talent, we started small with ad-hoc grants to fund equipment and training for students. As time went on, we realized our students could actually provide a service to the global chain, by performing and producing music that can be used across all their platforms and channels, including their restaurants. This allows for the partnership to be more sustainable over time, since there's a tangible return for the brand and a business model for our beneficiaries, whilst also building their own musical identity. That's resulted in a yearly partnership for us, which ensures *our community leaders and students can be part of something sustainable, creative and connecting for years to come.'*

INSTAGRAM: @BRIDGESFORMUSIC

Ways to raise: Twenty more cash-generating ideas for charities and non-profits

1. **Online auction** Sell art, crafts, vintage stuff, experiences, meals out – basically anything appealing (it can't be crap, otherwise people won't bother coming back) – to the highest bidder. You'll need mobile bidding software and some sexy stuff to auction, but there's lots of support online.

2. **'Donate' buttons on your website** Have a donation page on your website that makes your ask really compelling, with simple options for one-off or monthly donations. If you don't have a website, add a PayPal or Patreon link to your social media accounts.

3. **Email campaign** This is a more traditional way of asking your supporters for money, and you're no doubt very familiar with their tone and style as a result of getting lots of them in your inbox. Notice which stand out and why, and try to replicate the best. You'll need an email list; read more about how to get one on page 182.

4. **Social media challenges** Depending on the size of your platform (how many followers and supporters you are able to communicate with), a social media challenge could be a

fun way to get awareness going and link it to a fundraising campaign. Remember the Ice Bucket Challenge? It raised millions ... although studies showed that, in the UK, only around 10 per cent of people who took the challenge followed through with a donation.[11]

5. **Give while you shop or scroll** Many online shopping sites and social media platforms have a 'donate to charity' option, but you'll need to be a registered charity to enrol for these.

6. **Time-sensitive appeals** There's nothing like a sense of urgency to inspire people to donate to your cause, so if there's a key date or particular deadline for your project, make sure to communicate that to your supporters.

7. **Text-to-give** A way for smartphone-using supporters to donate by text. You don't even need their phone numbers for it to work, you can just send out a bespoke link. It hones the donation process by getting rid of the need to use a computer or even old-school direct mail, but you may just be able to achieve the same results by sending out a PayPal link.

8. **Online mentorship auction** Similar to the online auction, only this time you're auctioning off time with talented people – mentors, coaches, CEOs – anyone you can persuade to donate their time.

9. **Gigs** There's a lot of effort involved in putting on a gig, but if music is your thing and you are super-organized and energetic, it can work. You'll need to beg or borrow as

much as possible to keep your costs down, or find an event sponsor to cover the costs so that you can make money from the ticket sales.

10. **Film screenings** This can be a great way to fundraise for your cause, especially if you're screening films or documentaries that are relevant to it. We raised about £4,000 ($5,500) in one night through a local film screening, although that did include bar sales and a raffle (see idea number 11).

11. **Raffles** Who doesn't love a raffle? Until the moment all the prizes have been given away and you go away empty-handed … But still, they're a sure-fire way to raise cash for a good cause if you get some good prize donations. Creative peeps could come up with an 'everybody wins' model, but if not, at least the losers know their money is powering positive change.

12. **Gala dinners** A conventional and often lucrative way to raise funds if you've got a good network of wealthy individuals and/or business leaders – but you'll need to be a charity to make the most of it (because people who have lots of money to give to good causes tend to want to claim tax relief on their donation). Do make the event itself as sustainable as possible; they're notoriously guzzly in terms of resources.

13. **Community garage sale/flea market** This can be a fun and joyful community-building event. If you can persuade your neighbours or local community centre to get involved, it's a pretty low-maintenance, pleasurable way to raise cash. See how many houses or apartments you can get

involved, make sure they're happy to donate the proceeds of their second-hand treasures to your cause, set the date and promote it via flyers or local WhatsApp groups.

14. **Community supper clubs** This is similar to the garage sale idea, only this time your neighbours or people in your community agree to host a few people (or more if they're sassy in the kitchen) for dinner and people make a donation to come, as they would in a restaurant. It does require the host to pay for food, though, so you might want to come to an agreement that allows them to cover their costs, with any extra coming to your mission.

15. **Corporate gift-matching** If you've got good links with large, successful businesses, explore a corporate gift-matching programme. Their employees make a donation to your cause, and the company they work for matches the donation.

16. **Real handwritten letters** In a world where most people crave time away from screens and miss the good ol' days of getting post that wasn't just a boring bill or statement, a handwritten letter can be pure gold. Getting people's addresses is harder, but you can always write to them with your request via their agent or office.

17. **Restaurant partnerships** These are a nice way to build awareness of your mission in your home town or city, and can be a simple method of raising a steady trickle of donations. Basically, you get local restaurants (or one good one) to donate a percentage from each meal, or sometimes from a particular dish on the menu, to your cause. Try to

find restaurants that fit your values, for example someone fighting for animal rights would be better suited to the local vegan burger joint than a steakhouse.

18. **Silent auction** In person or online, these auctions offer art, craft, experiences, vouchers and so on, without the public element of bidding against someone. In a physical setting, the items are placed around the room and people write down their highest bid, then submit it to the organizers. Online, it's a similar process, just not as much fun.

19. **Clothes swap** Raise funds and save the planet at the same time! People *love* a clothes swap (we've had people queuing up for City to Sea ones) and are happy to pay for entry, especially if it's for a good cause. The deal is that they bring a bag of clothes to swap (ideally dropped off before the event, so that you have time to sort them and hang them up nicely), and can then take a bag of 'new' clothes away with them. You can make it more of an event by programming speakers or musicians.

20. **Sponsored anything** Ask people to sign up to a sponsorship site (of which there are loads) to raise cash from their community by doing a sponsored something. Cake bakes, cycle rides, shaving heads, burpees – so many things can be sponsored if someone's game. Sites such as JustGiving and GoFundMe offer ways for people to promote their fundraiser and process the donations.

SEAWILDING: SALTY TEARS, NATIVE OYSTERS AND SEAGRASS

As with most of Scotland's beautiful coastline, Loch Craignish has suffered significant degradation and destruction through scallop-dredging, salmon-farming and polluting run-off from industrial agriculture. The red-beanie-wearing ex-BBC journalist Danny Renton decided this was his calling, and the upset and injustice he felt at this ongoing environmental tragedy prompted him to found Seawilding in 2020. His work on documentaries for BBC Scotland and his climate-change studies had given him the awareness of both the problem and the solution, and were the catalyst for his brave jump from a stable job into the unknown, unpaid for 18 months while he worked out how to rewild the seabed.

Danny carried out a pilot project to prove it was possible to restore biodiversity in the loch using native oysters, which filter the water. With £800 ($1,000) in grant money from Sea-Changers (sea-changers.org.uk) to fund it, Danny bought oysters and cages and monitored them in the loch for a year. The project triggered lots of local interest, including a consultation in the town hall, giving him the support to start Seawilding with the aim of scaling up his efforts to enable the rewilding of many more of Scotland's beautiful lochs.

... one day, in a café in Edinburgh, he got the email that would change dozens of lives, and lochs

With this momentum, Danny submitted a substantial funding proposal to the National Lottery for £225,000 ($285,000). It was *a nail-biting wait to hear if he'd been successful, but one day, in a café in Edinburgh, he got the email that would change dozens of lives, and lochs. It was a pivotal moment for Seawilding; the grant would pay for one million oysters, an oyster nursery with floating cages, and an educational partnership to allow MSc students to survey the restoration efforts. The progress it allowed Seawilding to make also attracted a £75,000 ($105,000) donation from the Esmée Fairbairn Foundation, providing Danny with seed money for new projects for Seawilding and a modest salary for him and two more on his team for the next three years.*

Despite being a fledgling organization, Seawilding is well on its way to achieving Danny's ambitious goals, and more. Pollution and disturbance of habitat have resulted in the disappearance of 95 per cent of seagrass meadows in the UK's waters, so the Scottish government, through the NatureScot Biodiversity Challenge Fund, has now also pledged £145,000 ($190,000) to Seawilding to set up a seagrass restoration project. Danny is finding increasingly creative funding strategies, including promotions to sponsor 1 metre (3 ft) of seagrass restoration for £20 ($25), or an oyster cage for £130 ($170).

In encouraging others, like you, to take action when they see environmental or social problems in their community, Danny has two main pieces of advice. Firstly, 'Never sniff at any donation', because the more donors you have, the more confidence you give to other funders. He's clear that it was the original £800 grant that made his entire project possible. Second, 'It's impossible unless you have local buy-in.' He believes the first step to lasting change is making sure it's embraced – and wanted – by the local community.

I had the pleasure of asking Danny about his funding journey (and a lot more) while he rowed me out to see the oyster nursery in the summer of 2021. His boat got stuck on the way in to pick me up, so I had to take my jeans off and wade out to him in my pants. Quite a way to start an interview!

RESOURCES

* Jeff Brooks, *The Fundraiser's Guide to Irresistible Communications: Real-World, Field-Tested Strategies for Raising More Money* (2012)
* Scott Harrison, *Thirst: A Story of Redemption, Compassion and a Mission to Bring Clean Water to the World* (2018)
* More Onion: www.more-onion.com
* National Council of Nonprofits: www.councilofnonprofits.org
* The School for Social Entrepreneurs: www.the-sse.org
* UnLtd: www.unltd.org.uk

People

The people you work alongside aren't just key to the success of your mission, they're essential to the learning and growth you experience along the way. Doing good and getting paid isn't only about the externalities – the impact you have in the world achieving your goal – it's also about doing good by the people you attract, employ and serve.

There have been times at City to Sea when I got that wrong, times when I put the success of the mission before the success of the team. Ultimately, doing good 'out there' is undermined if you're not doing good (leading by example, prioritizing well-being, championing diversity) on the inside. Choose your people well, or, if they choose you in the early days when you can't afford to pay anyone, make sure you look after them.

The areas to consider when thinking about your people depend on your structure and the nature of your project. If it's just you on a mission to freelance your way to a brighter future, your people are probably few: maybe just you, some virtual assistants (note, these are still real people), and your friends and family, who keep you sane. But if you're setting up a charity or social enterprise, there will be a load of people in your orbit who may need hiring, firing, developing, training and nurturing. Here are some of them:

Board

There are generally two kinds of board to consider, depending on whether you're operating as a charity or a social enterprise. Charities legally require a board of trustees, and they make up the governing body that has overall responsibility for the organization's operations. Limited companies and social enterprises are only legally required to have one member and one director, and these can be the same person. However, since you're in business for the wider good of your community or planet, it's good practice to have at least three directors.

Boards are incredibly useful. Most non-profits have a board of non-executive directors, NEDs, who are (usually) unpaid experts in their field, helping to ensure the organization meets its legal obligations and operates within the law. They can also help you to set the strategy and ensure that it's delivered, contributing valuable advice, contacts and creativity. A diverse board can bring perspectives that are missing from your team, as well as experience and insight that help you to better understand and serve the communities you're aiming to support. Also, grant funders are a lot more likely to support you if you have a diverse membership or board, including people who have 'lived experience' of the problems you want to solve. Ideally your board will involve people from the communities you're working with, whether geographic locations or people with a shared interest.

The more board members you have, the more thorough oversight, expertise and transparency you'll have. Don't get carried away and have a massive board, though, or you'll spend most of your time talking to them, sending emails and trying to coordinate diaries. Five or six board members is the sweet spot for a small organization, and no more than 10-12 for a large one. Also, if you're asking for their opinions or sign-off, the more board members you have, the more difficult and time-consuming it is to make decisions.

UnLtd's helpful online guide 'Determining the Right Legal Structure for your Social Enterprise' sums up the board selection process nicely: 'You need to strike the right balance in terms of enabling diversity of viewpoints and perspectives while maintaining a nimble and decisive business.'[12]

Advisory board

Setting up a separate advisory board is a great way to bring in people with wide experience, skills and expertise to guide your operations and impact – without necessarily having to pay them. They can help you and the other senior member of your team see things differently, can provide impartial critical thinking, help you solve problems, and make valuable connections and introductions. Unlike a board of directors, who are legally responsible for the control, direction, governance and management of an organization, an advisory board – free from financial responsibility (called fiduciary duties) – can provide the specialist expertise you might not have or be able to afford on your team. In return for building up your confidence and skills and helping you achieve your mission, they get to play their part in changing the world.

Look at the people who are already supporting you. Do you have the makings of an advisory board around you? Write down the kind of support you have, and what you think you're lacking. Perhaps you still need legal expertise, funding support or campaigning insight. Once you're clear about what you need, get out there and make connections, asking experts you admire or who have been recommended if they'd be willing to help you make great stuff happen.

As well as having the most wonderful, wise advisors and mentors supporting our work at City to Sea, I also act as an advisor to others. I've been on advisory boards for Bristol Advisory Committee for Climate Change, supported Flight Free UK with campaign and recruitment advice, and helped the Launchpad Collective set up as a non-profit supporting refugees get ready for work. It can be hugely rewarding for the people who are helping you, so don't be afraid to ask for help.

Mentors and coaches

No matter how brilliant you are, there will always be gaps in your knowledge and expertise. Having talented people around you, or at the end of the phone, who are experts in their field and who care about you and your mission is pure gold. Whether they take the form of an official coach or business mentor or just a few informal relationships, I wholeheartedly recommend that you invest in and build your support network.

Look at the people who are already supporting you.

It's only now, looking back, that I see that the allies and mentors I had in the early days were in fact an unofficial advisory board. From funding advice to industry expertise or just founder-to-founder support, I don't think City to Sea would have succeeded without the people who advised me, mostly for free, when I was getting started. And over the past four years my business mentor has been my rock, my most trusted advisor and an unending source of inspiration and advice.

Business coaches are the bomb. When else do you get undivided attention from someone whose only purpose at that moment is to make your life and business better? A good business coach acts as a mirror, only they reflect your potential. If you're willing to grow and change, they'll help you get to where you want to be in the swiftest and easiest way possible. A business coach can also help you to be clear about what you really need, as well as what you want. It's definitely worth paying for if you can afford it. (If you can't, look up coaching academies whose trainees are seeking case studies and experience.) No one else will push you gently outside your comfort zone to see what you're capable of, while holding you accountable and encouraging you at every step.

Team

The sooner you're able to delegate work, the quicker you'll grow your business and increase your impact. Having people to work alongside you frees you to focus on the areas you're best at, be that fundraising, campaigning, talking to people or making art.

If you're not rolling in cash, and you're not sure for how long you'll be able to afford to pay someone, start by using freelance staff on an hourly rate or by project. You'll have fewer obligations to them as an employer (you'll just need an MOU – memorandum of understanding – and a contract), and both sides can be fairly flexible. Freelancers are quite easy to find if you advertise the contract on your networks, or you can use platforms such as Fiverr or Upwork to attract people at very competitive rates. From admin to accounts, social media support to filmmaking, freelancers can be a good way to start building your team.

Having people to work alongside you frees you to focus on the areas you're best at

Once your business or non-profit is in a more secure financial position, it makes sense (from a financial and ethical perspective) to employ people. You'll need to get your head around your legal obligations, such as minimum wage, employers' liability insurance, criminal-record or other suitability checks (particularly if working with young or vulnerable people), registering with the tax authority and setting up a workplace pension scheme. If you started glazing over or hyperventilating with panic reading that, a very cool tool for new businesses in the USA is the Small Business Administration (SBA), which can take you through everything from launching to managing to growing your business. In the UK there's the Federation of Small Businesses (FSB), to which you pay a small annual fee (around £177) in exchange for access to heaps of support, advice and helpful people who'll do this stuff for you. Magic.

Legal stuff aside, your people will be the most important aspect of your mission. They'll be your allies, your crew, your teachers and your challengers. They'll end up being the reason you keep going, they'll feed the fires when you've lost your spark, and they'll keep the values alive and fresh. So recruit the best, brightest, most brilliant people you can find, and do whatever you can to keep them.

Volunteers

When your mission is clearly social or environmental, involving volunteers can be a meaningful way to reach your goals, build community and increase your impact. Volunteers can help with all sorts of activity, including organizing events, conducting research and helping with digital marketing. For some, it's a way of gaining new skills and having real-world experience in the workplace, so you may attract students who are on a gap year, looking for experience in their holidays, or fresh out of university and seeking a way into work. Other volunteers might be retired or have had careers and raised kids and want to put their time and skills to good use. And, of course, there are the people who believe in what you believe in and will make time to help you, either in order to meet others on the same mission, or to feel as though they're making a difference.

When you have a project that could do with extra support, write out a simple job description. Include an idea of time commitment and location, and a list of essential and desirable skills. Then put a shout out on your social networks and share it with national and regional websites and newsletters that might also advertise it for you, such as LinkedIn or Volunteer Centre Finder.

Get off to a good start by creating a simple volunteer agreement, and develop a policy about how you'll work with volunteers so that the arrangements are clear and transparent. Set up your policies and systems to ensure you're keeping people safe and managing risk, safeguarding, and prioritizing the health, well-being and protection of volunteers *and* your group or the organization.

It's worth going the extra mile to be inclusive and welcoming to encourage the involvement of a wide range of people. Have a proactive approach to increasing volunteer diversity, addressing under-representation and including targeted groups as part of your inclusion, equity and diversity aims. Don't fall into the trap of being too busy to prioritize this, or you may end up with a single stream of privileged, well-educated volunteers whose parents are able to support them financially while they get work experience.

Once you've found good volunteers, look after them well. They're not being financially rewarded, so it's hugely important that they feel valued and that the benefits of their volunteering – and the impact they're having – are understood and communicated. Your volunteers are quite possibly the reason you're able to make progress, so at all times they should feel supported and a part of your organization, and that their contribution makes a difference.

Interns

Another way to get people power at a discounted rate is to offer internships. It can be a win-win, since you get the support you need and your intern gets to apply the skills they've acquired at college or university. Graduates who had a relevant job or internship while studying are more than twice as likely to acquire a good job immediately after graduating, so it's a worthwhile thing to do.[13] But internships are often abused by large corporations and media companies as free labour, and are usually grossly unfair in terms of

Aim to empower, not exploit

excluding people from middle- or working-class backgrounds; wealthier students gain access to internships, while the voices of low-income and minority groups are further marginalized. Aim to empower, not exploit, by offering paid internships or partnering with university programmes that offer paid internships to students from low-income backgrounds. You might also want to check out some of the paid-internship platforms online.

Collaboration

Collaboration is something that everyone talks about but few get right. We know it's important for many good reasons: to maximize our impact, reduce our costs, build our resilience … and anyway, duplication is for dummies. It's what our funders, staff and customers all want to see, so why is it so difficult to pull off? Well, we know in theory that it makes sense, but in practice it isn't that easy. We're busy, we've got our own ways of doing things, and getting it right can sometimes feel like it's slowing things down. There's also the problem of people or organizations with similar missions going for similar funding pots, which – in the old patriarchal paradigm of scarcity and competition – can be too much of a blocker to navigate. I've found that laying down clear ground rules can help. Here are my tips for making your collaborations come together in the most juicy, delicious way:

1. Take the time to develop your shared purpose and objectives in a creative and facilitated environment. Check out dancing-fox.com if you need help with that.

2. Create a simple Memorandum of Understanding (MOU) for how you'll work together and how you'd like to communicate with each other.

3. Embrace and embody the feminine principles (whatever your gender) of abundance, reciprocity, interconnectedness and vulnerability in your approach.

4. Define your shared values and goals, and communicate them joyfully to everyone involved.

5. Be clear on the funding allocation and different team roles – and how you'll deliver the work together.

6. Be transparent. If things go wrong or get delayed, honesty is the best policy.

7. Have fun. For the love of doing good and getting paid, take time to get to know and like each other, and have a blast along the way

When we get collaboration right, it can really accelerate our growth, credibility and impact. It gives you access to new people, skills and clients that could take years to develop by yourself. So it's well worth putting the energy and time into making it a success.

However, let's not gloss over the tough times. As with any relationship, there will be bumps in the road, and sometimes the road might even come to an end. There's no shame or blame in recognizing that something has failed or run its course; in fact, it's infinitely better to be honest and face the music sooner rather than later. If something isn't working and you've tried to fix it, trust your gut and move on. Just do it as honourably and courageously as possible, and stay on good terms. None of you – or the people around you, or the planet – need the stress. Save your precious energy for the good stuff.

HR

Healthy Relationships. Happy Radicals. Human Resources. Apparently, one of the main reasons start-ups fail is because teams are unhappy and fall out. That's really sad, because it's avoidable. But because it's such a big thing, the relationships between the individuals involved and their track record at delivering successful projects together is one of the main things investors and funders look at. They want to know you're not going to have a row and walk away when things get tough. So, if you're starting your own business, get your recruitment and management systems in place from the outset, to save you headaches down the line. It's also a great idea to embed really meaningful, tried-and-tested tools in your organization from the start, such as non-violent communication, radical candour and regular check-ins.

It's massively rewarding when you see people on your team thriving inside and out.

Get the policy stuff and handbooks in place (more on that on page 188), take time to write proper job descriptions, follow legal recruitment procedures and use formal employment contracts from the beginning. If in doubt, get free legal advice or sign up to the SBA or the FSB. There is lots of great information online, too.

Once you've found your dream employee, or built your dream team, you'll want to hold on to them. Recruitment is a costly and time-consuming process, and you want to build and grow talent, not lose it. Make sure you put the time into training people properly, have regular meetings and reviews, and keep piling on the praise when they're doing a good job.

HR can be a culture, not just something you go to when you need to raise a concern or sort out your paternity leave.

We're incredibly proud of our approach at City to Sea, probably because our HR manager, Hetti Dysch, shaped her own role, so it ended up being pretty unconventional. As a result, our team say they've never had HR so good.

Health and well-being

Running a time-sensitive campaign or starting a small business can be challenging for everyone involved, so it's important to consider how to prioritize people's health and well-being. You and your staff are your greatest and most precious assets, so there's a strong business case for investing in workplace health. Consider how you can support health and wellness, and make it a core part of your company values. It's massively rewarding when you see people in your team thriving inside and out. There's a whole section on page 192 on how to look after yourself when campaigning or leading a business, but for now here are a few simple tips for the workplace:

✳ Provide easy access to healthy food and drinking water at work.

✳ Encourage staff to exercise by organizing group fitness sessions or yoga classes (we have three budding yoga teachers at City to Sea, and they've always been happy to offer free sessions before work).

✳ Promote active travel to work, such as walking and cycling.

✳ Set up a mentoring programme so that staff can support each other, or so they have someone they trust to talk to outside the organization.

✳ Implement duvet days or mental-health days, so that people can take time out to look after themselves if they're feeling overwhelmed or anxious or just need time to process something.

HERA HUSSAIN: HOW VOLUNTEERS ARE BREAKING THE CHAYN

Founded in 2013 by Hera Hussain, Chayn ('solace' in Urdu) is a global non-profit run by survivors of gender-based violence and allies from around the world. It creates resources to inform and support the healing of survivors and to empower women against violence and oppression. From its roots as a volunteer-only initiative surviving on small donations and grants, to a network of over 400 volunteers worldwide with backing from supporters such as Comic Relief and the UK Department of Culture, Media & Sport, her leadership has created a truly impactful organization.

Hera's experience supporting two friends out of abusive marriages showed her the stark lack of support for survivors of gender-based violence, particularly multicultural and non-English-speaking women. Motivated to change this situation, she also wanted to create something without the typical corporate barriers to volunteer and staff involvement, such as qualifications and experience. This, combined with the diminishing funding for initiatives in the social sector, inspired her to set up Chayn as a volunteer-led organization, able to resist funding pressure and maximize inclusivity as a community. And it's phenomenally impressive. She found the first volunteers through advertising in feminist groups she was part of; these groups boosted Chayn's presence and got its work noticed. To this day, the only criteria volunteers must meet is having the time to get involved and a non-discriminatory mindset. Hera explains that one volunteer had withheld her views until leaving Chayn, at which point she revealed that the prejudices she'd come with had eroded so much during her time in the community that she felt like an entirely new person. All. The. Feels.

Chayn now has an incredible global volunteer base of over 400, at every level from governance to administration, 70 per cent of whom are survivors of gender-based violence. As well as helping others, it can rebuild the volunteers' self-esteem; many were told by their abusive partner that they could never do anything by themselves, yet are now leading projects for the organization. The flexible business model, where volunteers commit for just three or four months at a time, allows the community to avoid pressurizing its members and encourages new people to join. This is also achieved by Chayn's commitment to community-driven decision-making, whereby volunteers are invited to operational and strategy meetings – including board and budget meetings – and encouraged to give input. Hera's truly inspirational leadership can be seen in the dedication of her team. When she distributed a particularly heavy workload to them for a recent project, they were happy and keen to get stuck in, and didn't even realize the work would be paid until they received their contracts. That's love!

Hera's advice to anyone wanting to do good and get paid is to manage the power dynamics within the team or organization, promoting a 'relaxation of hierarchy' and reinforcing the members' shared interests. She also emphasizes the benefit

Chayn's flexible structure has had in preventing volunteers from having to choose between this commitment and their daily lives. By consistently asking herself 'What does an open and warm community look like?', Hera has created one in Chayn.

INSTAGRAM: @CHAYNHQ

Diversity

When I'm asked what I could have done differently with City to Sea, my response is generally 'diversity'. It wasn't until the end of 2018, well into our third year as a non-profit, that I realized our operations and output had become (or had always been) very white. Out of 300 applicants for all our advertised positions in 2016–18, only four had been from People of Colour, and three of those were Indian men (still based in India) applying for a software developer role. We hired the fourth, a British Asian woman based in Brighton. I remember thinking things like 'This is a reflection of the environmental movement in general' and 'I hardly ever see Black or Brown people at environmental events in Bristol'. I took it as the norm, even though I wasn't comfortable with it, and assumed People of Colour and those from marginalized communities were busy fighting their own battles for social justice.

On the 'Work for Us' page of our website was a paragraph saying, 'Although we treat all applications equally, we particularly welcome applications from male applicants and people from a BAME background' (we had, and still have, a lot of women working at City to Sea). My thinking was that if we made it clear that we wanted more People of Colour on our team, we'd suddenly, magically start attracting a more diverse pool of applicants. I didn't stop to think that perhaps I needed to dig a little deeper, to question my own ideas and assumptions about race and the systemic barriers that might be affecting the representation of minority groups in the environmental movement. I believed I didn't have time for that; I was too busy saving the world from plastic pollution to think about anything else. Racism, ableism – these were whole other topics that people working in social justice were dealing with anyway. Right?

When I'm asked what I could have done differently with City to Sea, my response is generally 'diversity'.

By 2019 I had realized that the 'we really want People of Colour to work here' message wasn't cutting it. Back then we had about 30 staff, and still the team was 94 per cent white. I started to pay more attention to the fact that the people who were applying for jobs – and those who were actively knocking our doors down to work with us – were young white women who'd studied some kind of marine biology, travelled the world, dived or surfed. They were talented, caring, passionate and privileged. Something started to click. With a new CEO at the helm, I had space to reflect. I was able to look up from my laptop and say to our HR manager: 'What are we actually doing about our lack of diversity? What is the sector doing about it?' More importantly, I had time to reflect on what I could be doing about my own lack of understanding. I'd never even heard the term 'intersectional environmentalism', and I'd never educated myself about privilege, power and unconscious bias. So was it any surprise that the organization I'd created was a reflection of that?

We set up a Power and Privilege working group and outlined a strategy. We reached out to organizations that could help us. We read articles and paid diversity consultants for advice and training, and we continue to educate ourselves and be part of the conversations happening across the environmental sector in the UK. And I personally started doing the work, reading books, attending training and finally acknowledging my own racism and biases.

I can't change the past, but if I could, I would have started my anti-racism and decolonializing education 20 years ago. What I can do now is not continue to make the same mistakes, to help others not make the same mistakes, and to continue to learn to be a better ally, or even accomplice. You might not be a 40-something-year-old white woman who grew up in a sea of white supremacy in suburban southern England. But there's a high chance, if you're reading this book, that you're white and privileged. I hope this chapter can help you learn from my mistakes and understand that you need to bake diversity and intersectionality into your project or campaign – and into yourself – from the beginning.

Diversity isn't just about race

Other things to consider if you want to create a truly diverse workplace or inclusive campaign include gender, sexual orientation, ability, age, socio-economic background and class. We need only look to nature to see that a rich tapestry of interconnected species is necessary for a healthy ecosystem. The plants need the intricate mycelium networks that run like tiny neural pathways through the soil, the soil needs the microbes and the worms, the birds depend on the worms and insects, the plants depend on the birds and insects to pollinate and spread their seeds, and so on and so on. Take away any aspect of the whole and the ecosystem will start to collapse.

Our campaigns and companies must also reflect this appreciation of wildness and fluidity. It will inevitably mean doing things differently from what people are used to if they come from a homogenized corporate workspace. If you're planning on growing a team, co-create your Diversity and Inclusion policy at the start, and embed and embody it in your operations and your content.

Tips for doing diversity better

✴ Start with your own board and/or management team. Having Diversity and Inclusion or Power and Privilege values and policies that you co-create, agree on and sign up to means that you make decisions and set up systems and processes that will actively start to create change.

✴ Recruitment is an important area to focus on if you want real change within your campaign or organization. Lots of recruitment processes are implicitly biased, so explore other ways of doing it, such as drawing up an initial values-based longlist of candidates rather than the traditional shortlist.

Other areas to consider include writing an inclusive job description, getting help to advertise the role through diverse networks, and shortlisting CVs with the personal information taken out.

✳ Take time to develop meaningful partnerships with organizations that are run by and/or for the people you are trying to attract. Spend time meeting and talking with them to learn what they do and how your work might be relevant to their customers, members or beneficiaries. Perhaps by putting on joint events – or just promoting each other's work – you can start to develop a better understanding of and credibility with the people you want to serve, which will ultimately help you to create a more diverse and inclusive environment, content and communications.

✳ Think about your communication and sign-up forms. Are the language and options appropriate in terms of ethnicity and gender? Is your application process accessible? Do your social media posts include captions for the visually impaired? Are you using the right terminology? These change regularly, so keep learning and stay current.

✳ Pay people fairly for their time and expenses, or be transparent from the outset about what you can offer in exchange for their work.

✳ Make events inclusive; be considerate of timing (for example, working parents – especially single ones – will need to find childcare for evening events), location and accessibility.

✳ Be patient and be kind. Hundreds of years of injustice and trauma won't be resolved in your five-year strategy. But make a commitment and keep nourishing it.

Other things we did and that you can do

✳ Set up a working group among your team or volunteers to keep flying the flag for diversity and inclusion and pushing for change inside and out.

✳ Support the redistribution of power and take part in initiatives such as #PassTheMic, which is working to amplify the voices of those on the front lines of the climate crisis and climate campaigning.

✳ Keep learning. We put a weekly half-hour slot in the team's diary for reading and reflection on power and privilege.

✳ If you're white, and you're invited to speak on an all-white, non-disabled panel, ask the organizers about their selection process. If they can't invite any more people, stand down and make suggestions for alternative speakers from a minority group.

✳ Diversify your input and output. Make sure you're reading and following people from under-represented communities and amplifying their stories in your content.

✳ Set up a 'brave space' at work. We have a weekly 40-minute group circle to share our learnings or ask questions about diversity and inclusion as well as social and environmental justice.

✳ Research the use of pronouns (they / them, she / her, he / him) and decide whether you'd like to include them in your email signatures or social media profiles.

RESOURCES

* Diversity and Ability: diversityandability.com
* Intersectional Environmentalist: intersectionalenvironmentalist.com
* Sue Unerman, Kathryn Jacob and Mark Edwards, *Belonging: The Key to Transforming and Maintaining Diversity, Inclusion and Equality at Work* (2020)
* Arthur Woods and Susanna Tharakan, *Hiring for Diversity: The Guide to Building an Inclusive and Equitable Organization* (2021)

Activities and impact

Whether you're setting up your own organization or approaching your mission as a side hustle, it's likely that you'll want to run a campaign. Sometimes, what starts as a campaign grows into an organization – Extinction Rebellion is a good example – but it's common for campaigns to be run independently and wrap up once they've achieved their goal. This section is designed both for campaigning as part of an organization and for the lone wolves ready to tear up the status quo from their bedrooms.

What is a campaign?

A campaign is a defined project that focuses on a particular goal or outcome. It's created to bring about a specific change, such as getting the government to adopt or change a law or policy, or stopping a road from being built through your local playground. Effective campaigning creates real-world change through influencing others and is the vehicle behind some of the biggest social and environmental changes we've seen in history. (Yup, it's not normally governments leading the changes

spend time getting your house in order before you act

we need to see in the world, it's everyday folk like you who are fighting for what you believe in.) So, you could say that campaigning is what makes the world a better place. Anyone can do it, but it helps to have a plan, a few tools and some resources at your fingertips.

Where to start?

If you're planning something epic, such as stopping a war or an airport expansion, you'll need to spend time getting your house in order before you act, essentially building a solid evidence base by doing research and conducting consultations, surveys and testimonials. To influence the people you're trying to change, you'll want to be able to demonstrate that you know your stuff, that your reasoning is sound and that your solution is robust.

Even if you're planning something smaller, it's still wise to do plenty of research and analysis before you launch, to check that your outcomes, if successful, won't have any unintended negative consequences. Let's take the invention of plastic as an example. In the nineteenth century the demand for billiard balls, which were made of ivory from elephant tusks, was so high that elephant populations were decimated. A decline from 26 million to 10 million African elephants was attributed to the production of billiard balls – along with piano keys, combs and brushes – between the mid-nineteenth century and the early twentieth.[14] Finally, the penny dropped and the billiards manufacturers realized their source wasn't sustainable. They ran a competition for a new material and celluloid, an early form of plastic, was the winner. It was little thought that this indestructible material that can last several lifetimes, although created to save wildlife, would become one of the biggest environmental pollutants of the twenty-first century. D'oh! We see the plastics and packaging industry in similarly dangerous territory these days with the switch from fossil-fuel-based plastic to bioplastic. While there's a place for plant-based 'hard' plastics (in gadgets and gizmos) and for single-use plant-based plastics (in closed-loop systems such as festivals and hospitals), creating another throwaway product from genetically modified crops that require land,

The more time you spend planning your campaign, the more effective it'll be

water and countless fertilizers and pesticides constitutes jumping out of the frying pan and into the fire.

So do your research, check for unintended consequences in terms of outcomes and switches, be confident with your evidence and get ready to implement your master plan.

SWOT up

Scope out the landscape around your campaign. Who's involved? Is anyone else campaigning on this? Who does it affect? Getting a handle on the forces at play will make your campaign stronger, inform your strategy and ward off any risks.

A SWOT (Strengths, Weaknesses, Opportunities and Threats) analysis is a classic piece of kit to have in your campaign toolbox. Basically, it's a framework to help you understand the different circumstances your campaign might face. You can consider things like funding, skills and resources, as well as your stakeholders, potential opposition and even curveballs such as a global pandemic. SWOTs are also helpful when it comes to organizing the information and research you've collected, and can help you start making decisions about your next steps.

If this kind of stuff floats your boat and you love geeking out on analysis, you can always throw a PEST (Political, Economic, Social and Technological) into the mix. I prefer a PESTLE, because it also includes Legal and Ecological ... let's not leave the planet out of these tools! PESTs help you get a sense of the driving forces around you and your campaign. It's essentially about the big picture and how that might affect you, your campaign or your organization.

Slogans are sexy, stories are seductive

Now define and design your campaign. What are you campaigning for? Do you have a realistic goal? Can you communicate it effectively? Catchy slogans, simple hashtags and a convincing story are essential for public-facing campaigns. People must be able to get your message in a flash, so keep it simple and accessible. But bear in mind that not all campaigns need to be public-facing. Sometimes you might be able to achieve your goals by putting pressure on groups, companies or government ministers. If this is the case, you can focus more on crafting the argument for change, and less on how it looks and sounds.

The more time you spend planning your campaign, the more effective it'll be – subject to the time and resources you have, of course. There are some fantastic free resources online around creating a campaign plan or strategy, and City to Sea's favourites are listed at the end of this section. If you're pressed for time and want to get cracking, here's an overview of campaign planning:

Who? People like people. Be ready to tell your story and why you're doing this campaign.

What? Boil down your campaign goal into one killer sentence. Make it clear, compelling and to the point. If you're looking for funding (more on that in a moment), you might also benefit from having a Theory of Change up your sleeve (see page 95).

How? Work out your tactics: who you need to influence and how you're going to reach them. Does your campaign lend itself to an online petition? Does it involve direct action such as protests and marches? Do you need money to make it happen? If so, head to page 120 to find ideas for raising the funds you need.

When? Create a strategy document that keeps you on track. Use this as your touchstone for the next thing you need to do and when.

Is it working?

As your campaign progresses, you'll need to assess how you're doing, both to track your progress and to see if you need to change anything, so make sure you've included monitoring and evaluation in your campaign plan. Monitoring is needed to demonstrate your progress. As well as actually achieving your campaign goal, you can also measure how many:

✳ People have signed your petition

✳ People have visited your website

✳ People have used your hashtag

✳ People got involved in your event/action/protest

✳ Media mentions you've had

✳ MPs have been contacted

✳ Discussions have been had in Parliament about your campaign issue

✳ New followers or sign-ups to your mailing list you've gained

Evaluating is mostly done at the end of a campaign, or at a milestone, to bring out the learnings and inform your next steps. You can also use your evaluation time to build in impact measurement. Your social and environmental impact is the positive change that you or your campaign or organization has made happen or influenced. If you're running a social enterprise or charity, creating positive change is your reason for being, so you'll need to have a really good handle on what change you've created and what value your activities have brought to nature or society (or both). The saying 'information is power' is totally relevant here, because as a campaigner or business your impact is your currency. It's what you need in order to show your stakeholders (your supporters, community and partners) and funders the impact they've had by supporting your campaign. And, if you're looking to attract more funding or investment, your impact is the nectar that will attract the honeybees. Or moneybees, in this case.

As well as measuring more obvious outcomes such as media reach, petition signatures and changes in legislation, you might want to explore measuring your social impact, especially if you're going for funding from grants, trusts, foundations or corporates. They'll want robust evidence that your theory of change works, and they'll want to know that their money is making a difference, something that is commonly called SROI (social return on investment). It's a world unto itself, and worth getting your head around if you're serious about building relationships with major donors and CSR initiatives. Check out socialvalueuk.org for an overview of SROI and how to measure it.

At City to Sea, we've got ACOs (annual company objectives) as well as an SROI model. Our ACOs keep the board and senior leadership on track with yearly goals around impact (how much plastic we've stopped from entering the waste stream), awareness (how many people we're reaching), accessibility (how much refill and reuse infrastructure we've enabled) and action (volume of individual and corporate behaviour change).

If developing ACOs or an SROI model feels a bit too detailed for your mission, stick to the basics. Your campaign plan will lay out your targets and desired outcomes, so keep checking how you're doing against those goals and don't forget to tell the people who matter how things are going.

THE ART OF GENTLE PROTEST

Sarah Corbett is a living, breathing campaign queen. But, unlike Boudicca, her army is one of knitters, stitchers, makers and crafters whose only weapon of mass destruction is a yarn bomb. She's the founder of Craftivist Collective, a social enterprise that helps people to engage in activism, or craftivism, in a 'quiet, non-confrontational manner involving pretty, handcrafted gestures of defiance'. And those gentle acts have resulted in pretty significant shifts for the better.

Take Sarah's involvement in getting Marks and Spencer (M&S) – one of the UK's leading retailers – to commit to paying workers the independent living wage. It began with an email in 2015 from the CEO of ShareAction (shareaction.org), an environmentally and financially focused campaigning organization. ShareAction had been trying to pressurize M&S to make this change before its Annual General Meeting in five weeks' time, but had not succeeded. ShareAction's CEO had read Sarah's book on craftivism and wanted to work with her to try a new way of protesting.

There are various ways that a gentle protest can be carried out at pace, such as street art, wearable symbols, community installations and shop-dropping (effectively reverse shoplifting, where you place specific things on shop shelves, such as art or labels). Sarah opted for giving gifts to the people with the power to make the change. She decided to make a unique handkerchief for each M&S board member, for each CEO of M&S's five largest investment companies, and for five celebrity models involved in M&S's recent campaign (including Rita Ora). She described her mission as becoming 'critical friends, rather than aggressive enemies', supporting those with power to use it positively. And, rather brilliantly, she called the campaign 'Don't Blow It'. Genius.

Sarah bought the 24 handkerchiefs from M&S, reasoning that M&S would be more likely to listen to a customer than to a stranger. (She was probably the first person under the age of 30 to buy a handkerchief from M&S in 50 years.) Her project gained exposure and Malala Yousafzai attended one of her workshops, but Sarah chose to use 24 less well-known craftivists to stitch the hankies, reinforcing her message that craftivism is open to everyone. The hankies were tailored to each target through researching their background, and each gift was delivered with a personal, handwritten letter.

During the campaign, Sarah also organized 'stitch-ins'. These were small picnics outside M&S stores around the country, where participants discussed their goals with customers and staff. Because of the unusual nature of this campaign, it gained a variety of media exposure, from newspapers to blogs admiring the picnic aesthetic. The editor-at-large of Time Out magazine *covered the campaign and supported it, describing the picnics as 'adorable'.*

Finally, the AGM arrived. In his introduction, the chairman (Robert Swannell) mentioned the campaign and said it had been carried out wonderfully. Sarah addressed the board, letting them know that the campaigners had brought gifts and wanted to meet them. This resulted in one-on-one meetings with all the board members, allowing the campaigners to understand who supported and opposed them with far more openness than if they'd confronted the board without having offered such meaningful gifts.

This led to three more meetings in the next 10 months, and resulted in M&S publicly committing to paying above the independent living wage by the time of the next AGM. Don't Blow It had won! After the meeting, the board members came to thank the campaigners for the gifts and said they had engaged only because of the campaign's gentle approach. The impact of the gifts was further revealed when one board member told Sarah she had taken her handkerchief home and been asked about it by her children, to whom she had to explain the wage issue.

Sarah's advice to you on forming campaign strategies? It's simple and beautiful: 'Figure out how to lift people up rather than push them down.' That's a philosophy that goes far beyond campaigning, don't you reckon?

INSTAGRAM: @CRAFTIVISTS

RESOURCES

* Campaign Bootcamp (now closed, but still has a huge amount of useful info online): campaignbootcamp.org/resources

* Nora Gallagher and Lisa Myers, *Tools for Grassroots Activists: Best Practice for Success in the Environmental Movement* (2016)
* Brian Lamb, *The Good Guide to Campaigning and Influencing* (2011)
* National Council for Voluntary Organisations: knowhow.ncvo.org.uk/campaigns
* Sheila McKechnie Foundation: smk.org.uk/what-we-do/training

Marketing

Whether you're setting up and running a new business, or ready to set the world on fire (er, or try to cool it down) with your campaign idea, you'll need to get it out there. For some people, marketing – the mechanism to get people to buy into your product, service or campaign – comes naturally. They're easy communicators, all over social media, comfortable in front of the camera, and love networking and making new connections. For others, marketing is an overwhelming proposition.

Remember that when you work for yourself, you are the brand.

They just want to do the tech bit, or the research bit, or get on with delivering the results and impact. Think about where you sit on that scale, and if you're not turned on by marketing, find someone who is. Without effective communications, without the petition signatures or the customers, the followers or the community, your mission is unlikely to succeed. It's that crucial.

So let's look at the basics you'll need to cover, from strategy to social media, so that you can make a plan for your mission. We'll focus on two areas, marketing your business or product and communicating your campaign.

Marketing your business

Before you start communicating with the world, or at least with the people you want to reach, spend some time defining your brand identity and tone of voice. According to Jo Morley, Queen of Comms (aka head of marketing and campaigns) at City to Sea, 'It's deciding who you are, what you stand for and how you want to be perceived by the world.' Basically, it's what she holds sacred, and when that stuff is well held, the rest takes care of itself.

Creating your brand
A brand is a lot more than a logo and colour scheme. It's your look, your feel, your values, your communications and how you show up in the world, all in one beautiful package. This is probably the one thing I'd recommend getting external help with, pro bono if you don't have the cash to pay someone. It's essential to find a good designer who's used to helping people create a visual identity that represents their mission. Of course, *you* might be that person; some people eat Photoshop, InDesign and Illustrator for breakfast and turn concepts into killer visuals.

Remember that when you work for yourself, you *are* your brand, and everything you do and say publicly is part of it. This means it's important to be clear on your purpose and values and to tell stories that reflect them. Also, it's 100 per cent worth investing in good-quality up-to-date photos of yourself and colleagues to use on your website and social media.

Knowing your audience
This is also known as targeting. The clearer you are about who you're trying to reach, the easier it'll be to develop a strategy to reach them. If it's wealthy females over 60, you're unlikely to need to invest in TikTok. If it's 16–25-year-olds, you might. Knowing your audience means you can create meaningful, resonant content that they will love, so take your time researching them: what media they read or use, where they spend their time and what they care about.

Communications
At a top level, your comms are how and where you communicate with your (now clearly defined) audience. From a business perspective, these are your potential clients or customers. Having these conversations has – in theory – never been easier, and there are many different ways to connect with people, across the huge range of online channels from social media platforms, email newsletters and chatbots to vlogs, blogs and podcasts.

However, in an increasingly busy online world it's vital to have a strong and consistent presence across whichever ones you choose to use, which – unless you want to overwhelm yourself and spread yourself verrrry thin – will be about three. The platforms or methods you choose will ideally be those where your customers and other people whom you want to influence will be hanging out. You need to be visible and to have a strong voice and message, with the aim of building and maintaining a great relationship with your customers and other stakeholders.

Social media

Love it or hate it, depending on who your audience is you're probably going to need to make friends with social media. It's very easy to spend a *lot* of time on it, so be strategic and focused in order to use your time well. Choose your platforms wisely and play to your strengths; you might need to put in a fair bit of effort to build a profile on there, so you may as well enjoy it.

Social media, if used well, is a massive opportunity. It's a free tool for you to use to communicate with your audience, so in theory it is as available to you as it is to any corporate brand. If you have a budget you can use it for paid advertising, too. This can be effective for a targeted campaign or launching a new product, but it isn't essential. What is important is that you have good-quality, consistent and authentic content that engages your audience and builds their trust.

Through having conversations with your ideal customers or supporters, you can find out where they are most likely to be. These are the top four to consider:

Instagram Probably the most popular for people between 25 and 45, and popular with influencers, brands, bloggers, small-business owners, friends and everyone in between, Instagram has well over 1 billion monthly users. It's quite reel-heavy these days, but photos and long-form captions still seem to be holding their own, so if you prefer a quieter, more gentle form, Instagram can work for you.

Facebook With nearly 2.5 billion monthly users, this is still the largest social media site in the world, so despite some of its questionable ethics and the fact that young people have largely moved away, it's hard to ignore. Facebook groups can be useful for building community; in fact, I'd go so far as to say that this is probably the main draw these days. If you start a page, you're going to have to pay to promote pretty much every post, so unless you've got a ton of cash behind you, go for groups over pages.

Twitter This is a good platform for connecting with other businesses and organizations, campaigners and activists, with around 350 million users. Some people love the short-form tweets, especially those with witty repartee and a love of banter. As with all social media platforms, it's troll-heavy, but it's still a good one to consider if you enjoy the upsides of Twitter. It's a great place for news, too, so it can be good for learning and staying up to date with what's happening in your space.

TikTok Hot on the heels of Facebook in terms of user numbers, TikTok has (at the time of writing) a massive 1.3 billion users. In 2020 about 25 per cent of UK teenagers and 70 per cent of US teenagers were using TikTok, which is incredible. Or terrifying, if you've watched the film *The Social Dilemma* (2020). TikTok is fast-paced, fun (if you like that kind of thing) and the perfect place for short-form video content.

LinkedIn This is still very much on the rise, and an increasingly popular and effective platform for connecting with people who'll be able to help you to develop and grow your work, whether as collaborators, funders, customers or other supporters. It's definitely an important place to be if you've got your business shizzle on. Take the time to create a great profile, share great content and connect with great people.

PR and media

PR (public relations) is important because it's all about reaching more people who might care about what you do and want to join you on your mission. Good PR harnesses the power of communication and media, which traditionally means press, TV and radio, although it can now include social media and influencers. It's a powerful tool when you get it right.

PR is a specialist area, though, and talented PR people tend to have built up long-standing relationships with journalists, so if you can, get early advice and support from people who know what they're doing. Perhaps you could persuade a PR specialist to join your advisory board? If not, PR is something you can learn on the job and reap big rewards from, even if you don't have a large budget. Journalists are looking for good content, so if you've got a great story, a local angle or a newsworthy event, send a well-written press release to your local media outlets or contact local journos on Twitter.

Other ways to generate PR and publicity are via social media or in-person events, speaking engagements or stunts. The best PR involves telling a story, ideally yours or that of the people, land or wildlife you're helping, to capture people's imagination. Practise telling yours, and tell it as often as you possibly can.

Awards

Another great way to get free publicity is by winning awards. There are lots of different ones to apply for each year, so watch out for those that are relevant to your work, for example social enterprise or campaign of the year, best sustainability initiative or green champion. A quick online search will bring up a range of options (try starting with awards-list.co.uk), but you'll need to check which charge an entry fee. Beyond publicity, awards also build credibility and confidence in your mission or project, which can be invaluable when it comes to securing funding.

If you're clear about your purpose, mission, brand and target audience, you're ready to invest in a good website.

Awareness days/weeks

National or global awareness days really help you get your message across. There should be a few that align with your mission – for example Earth Day, World Oceans Day and Mental Health Awareness Week. Have a scan through awarenessdays.com and make a list of those that relate best to your mission. As well as the smaller ones (British Tomato Fortnight, anyone?), there are lots of bigger annual initiatives that you could link to an event or campaign: for example, Fairtrade Fortnight or Organic September.

Awareness days are an easy way to amplify your message on social media; just make sure you use the right hashtags so that as many people as possible see your messages. Incorporate them into your annual social media content planner, so you can build your work and communication around them. A bit of forward planning can reap dividends in terms of free publicity, by raising awareness of your work among new audiences. Whatever happens, don't be tempted to jump on the bandwagon of someone else's awareness day to get coverage for yourself. Be authentic and respect other people's causes.

At City to Sea, we usually align with Earth Day, World Environment Day, World Oceans Day and World Menstrual Health Day. We even went a step further and created our own, World Refill Day, a global public-awareness campaign to get plastic pollution on the agenda and highlight reuse as the solution. In 2021, the year we took the campaign global: we had activity in 77 countries, reached over 168 million people through social media, and had an estimated potential media reach of over a billion. All that put the refill revolution firmly on the map.

Website

In an ever-changing, fast-paced digital world, websites are holding their own. Even apps seem to be transitioning back to web-based apps, so it's a good idea to invest in one early on. Your website helps people to find you, get in touch, read longer articles about your work, sign up to your mailing list, buy products … and the list goes on. If you're unsure whether you need one, or if you just want to register a brilliant domain name or get out some basic information, you can create a pretty simple, free website on platforms such as WordPress and Wix. (You'll need to pay for hosting if you're using your own domain name for the website and emails.)

If you're clear about your purpose, mission, brand and target audience, you're ready to invest in a good website. It'll make your life a lot easier and form an important marketing tool – think of it as your online 'brochure' or sales page that captures people's attention and makes them believe in you and your mission. Get recommendations from friends and businesses for a good web designer and web developer (often they'll be working together, but not necessarily). The designer makes it look sexy, the developer makes it work smoothly. Be prepared to invest in this part, because it's worth it in the long run.

Email marketing

This is done via your list of supporters' email addresses. Initially, it might just be you emailing friends and family to tell them about your mission. If that's the case, make sure you blind-copy everyone in the email so you're not sharing everyone's personal email addresses. But if you want to build a list that you can communicate with frequently – to ask them to get involved in action days or events, tell them about your progress, or ask for donations – it's worth using dedicated email mail-out software such as Mailchimp, HubSpot or Constant Contact. You'll need to make sure people opt in before you start emailing them, to ensure you are compliant with data-protection laws such as GDPR. An engaged email list is incredibly valuable if you want to continue building your organization, but not so important if your campaign is a one-off.

Emails work alongside social media, but you'll get a different, more focused form of attention from people reading an email than from those seeing a social media post, because they've actively invited you into their inbox – something that should be seen as a privilege in this busy ol' world. There are fantastic tools and training out there for improving your email communications; check out more-onion.com and charitydigital .org.uk for some great, free resources.

Endorsements and influencers
Like it or lump it, celebrity culture reigns supreme. People go mad for celebrities; a single Instagram post from someone famous can result in that product being out of stock

... celebrity culture reigns supreme.

the next day. Likewise, a famous person telling people to sign your petition or follow you on social media can supercharge your campaign. Choose influencers whom your audience trust and listen to, and who align with your mission. Ethical influencers are out there; most will charge a fee for supporting your work, but if they're really connected to your cause, they might not. See who's in your network, call in some favours and get some high-profile people flying your flag.

Communicating your campaign

If you're not marketing your business, you may well be marketing your campaign. Or – as we are at City to Sea – you may be in the business of marketing campaigns. Campaigns, whether carried out alone or as part of an organization's marketing strategy, have similar marketing needs to businesses, but with a campaign you're aiming for a specific result, usually within a certain time frame. That means you can use all the marketing tools and techniques outlined above, but tailor them to your campaign.

Start off by getting a comms strategy in place for your campaign. Include things like the over-arching campaign aims (objectives), how you're going to tell your story (key messages), who you want to reach (audience), how you're going to reach them (deliverables), and when this is going to happen (timeline). The more detailed, the better, so that you have a roadmap – aligned to your budget, if you have one – to get you from A (no one's heard of you or your campaign) to B (you bring down white supremacist capitalist patriarchy and the crowd goes wild).

Shooting from the hip and throwing away the rule book ...

All this is good to know if you want to get your work or project out into the world. But don't let it bog you down or bamboozle you. Feel free to innovate, disrupt and make shit up as you go along. Try stuff out, and if it works, do more of it. If it fails, don't do it again, or do it differently. Marketing is ultimately about connecting with people and persuading them to take action. It's totally up to you whether you do that through traditional forms or by running naked through the local mall scattering leaves hand-printed with your message.

Come to think of it, we did quite a lot of semi-naked stuff in the early days and it seemed to go down well. Don't overthink it, don't censor yourself, be inclusive and always, always be creative, baby.

RESOURCES

* FairSay: fairsay.com
* National Council for Voluntary Organisations: ncvo.org.uk
* Campaign Strategy: campaignstrategy.org
* CharityComms: charitycomms.org.uk

Admin

Stifle the yawns, hold the eye rolls and get your inner secretary juiced up and ready to admin the pants off your workflows. Or just learn about what you might need to delegate if you're really, really bad at being organized. Whether you thrive in chaos or are already super-efficient when it comes to tax returns and spreadsheets, you must get your workspace in order if you want to have a happy team, pay people, get paid, do what you said you were going to do, measure how well it went (and, if it failed, work out why), and create and share meaningful data that might help others solve similar issues.

Project management

Once you've developed your campaign plan or business model, you'll need a system to manage it effectively and stay (or get) organized. When things kick off and get busy, or if a curve-ball comes your way, you'll know what to do next if you've got project-management tools in place. Depending on your preferred working style, you can do this on a spreadsheet with an old-school Gantt chart (search 'how to create a Gantt chart' online for heaps of articles, advice and templates) or try one of the many excellent free project-management tools, such as Asana, Basecamp and Trello, all of which are especially useful when you're working in a team.

Get organized

There are lots of amazing online SaaS (Software as a Service) tools to help you save time and operate professionally as a small organization or business. These are centrally hosted and operate by subscription, although most offer free introductory packages. From accounting (more on that below) to social media scheduling (Buffer, ContentCal, Hootsuite, Later) and email marketing (Mailchimp, Hubspot, Keap), there's something out there for all your needs, and for needs you didn't even know you had. Take Slack, a messaging app for teams that can massively reduce that email mountain. Using software tools of this kind can save you time and money and enable you to scale your work effectively without having to hire people to help you. Another tool for saving time and energy is online meeting and scheduling software. I use the free version of Calendly, but there are loads to choose from – and it's been a revelation.

Look after your data

Back the fuck up. Seriously, make sure you are backing everything up, regularly. A simple way to make sure you don't lose your files and data is to keep things in the cloud, for example on Google Drive, Dropbox or OneDrive. This also makes it really easy to share files with anyone you work with and to access them from your phone or other devices. You can share folders with different people and edit in real time, which is useful when in a meeting or working on a project. But I don't even trust the cloud entirely, so we make sure our IT providers take regular back-ups too. Just ensure you're not storing a load of stuff you don't need. A big downside to storing files and data in the cloud is that it uses a serious amount of energy, so if you're using the cloud for storage, make space in your diary for regular digital decluttering. If possible, store the big stuff you don't need access to very often on hard drives that you can unplug.

Invoicing and accounting

The fun bit! Well, getting paid for doing good is definitely fun, but you'll need systems to make sure paying others and getting paid runs smoothly. Consider an online accounting tool such as QuickBooks, Xero or Sage, or look at the free ones, such as Wave, QuickFile and ZipBooks. Compare features and pricing to help you find the right one for you and your team.

If you're running or setting up a business, it's a very, very good idea to get an accountant. It's not a legal requirement (unless you're turning over more than £6.5 million, in which case you probably don't need to read this li'l book), but limited companies have forms to submit annually, as do CICs and charities. Unless you are confident managing these, as well as tax returns, it's worthwhile finding a spreadsheet god or goddess in human form who can nail it for you.

Set up a separate business bank account as soon as you can (ideally with an ethical bank such as Triodos or Starling). Keeping your business finances separate from your personal ones will make your annual accounting easier.

The law

We're nearly there with the boring-but-really-important stuff. I've been asked a lot about how to work with volunteers and what policies a new charity or social enterprise might need. So here goes. Maybe schedule a treat for when you get to the end of this section. I've done the same for writing it. (You will have guessed by now that story-telling and comms are way more interesting to me than the legal stuff.) But this bit is hugely important, because protecting your team, your board members and yourself is crucial for good governance and peace of mind.

Policies

Your organization's policies are the guidelines you develop to define your principles and processes. They establish good governance, lay out the rules of conduct (how you and your team strive to behave) and define how decisions must be made, or not made. As well as describing your responsibilities, they can create a frame of reference for handling everyday issues that arise when you're running or setting up an organization. They don't have to be massive essays; sometimes a couple of sentences will do.

Policies help to mitigate risk as well as communicate the individual and team responsibilities, enabling everyone to work together towards the company's objectives. When they are clearly written and easily understood, you'll be in a better position if you do get into legal territory or court challenges. Make sure yours are in place and up to date, make them available on your website and share them with your team and volunteers.

The good news is that you don't need to start from scratch, because there are lots of examples online. If you're strapped for time and your campaigns are careering ahead, consider finding an HR intern, volunteer or research student to help you get your policies sorted. Certain policies are a legal requirement if you're employing more than five people. These are:

✳ Equal opportunities

✳ Health and safety

✳ Equality and diversity

✳ Discipline/dismissal and grievance

… and if you're working with children, young people or vulnerable adults, you'll also need a safeguarding policy. Here are some others to consider:

Sustainability policy
This outlines your commitment to practices and standards that promote environmentally and socially responsible operations, so it's a no-brainer if you're all about doing good. Make it a simple, living document that expresses your commitment to the environment, and plant it deeply into your ways of working – across all departments – to make sure you stay on track. Ideally, keep a copy visible on your website and in physical spaces too, so that your team, supporters and clients can see it and be inspired by it too.

Privacy and personal data policies
You'll need this if you're collecting any kind of data on your website, such as mailing lists, payments or even data from website traffic (including Google Analytics). General Data Protection Regulations (GDPR) have been in place since 2018, meaning that you must comply with certain requirements relating to the management and storing of personal data. For support and examples, search online for 'data protection policy' or 'GDPR policy'.

Insurance

If you're trading, have a board or are running events with volunteers, you need insurance. Insurance policies can cover you, your business, your team and your volunteers against financial loss if anything goes wrong. An insurance claim will help towards the cost of compensation and legal fees you might be dealt in such a situation, and will also protect against damage and loss. You don't want to have to stop trading or campaigning because of a curveball that means you can't afford to carry on, so do take out appropriate cover. Here's a summary of the options:

Public liability
Covers you in case a member of the public is injured, or their property is damaged, as a result of your business activity. It's essential if you're doing events or actions.

Professional indemnity
Covers the cost of potential legal action if you offer professional advice or expertise to other businesses or clients.

Employers' liability
This is required only if you have one or more employees, so sole traders can operate legally without it.

Directors' and officers' liability
If you're a founder or director, definitely get directors' and officers' cover (D&O). Whereas the other policies cover the business itself, D&O protects the individuals responsible for that business: you, the board members, non-executive directors and people who have management responsibility. We all make mistakes, so having D&O insurance covers you for claims made against you personally.

Compliance

This is the system to ensure that you or your organization don't break the law and have the right policies and procedures in place. It sounds boring to some, but others get a kick out of making sure all the 'i's are dotted and the 't's crossed. Whatever the case, you gotta do it. Personally, I sleep better at night knowing the right people on our team are all over this. You'll need to stay up to date with laws and regulations to make sure you're compliant, but if this stuff gives you a headache, invest in help to keep you legal. Membership of the FSB or SBA is the best way to get support with compliance and make sure you're doing everything necessary.

You can also ask HR or legal advisors to join your advisory board, and keep an eye out for pro bono legal opportunities available to you as a charity or social business. For regular updates, register with a local business support body or council to find out about any changes and about relevant courses you can attend to find out more.

Self-care

Hey, friend. This is the bit where we take a breath together and go a bit deeper. It's all been quite heady so far, with lots of talk of funding, impact and the technicalities of running a campaign or business. But underneath it all, at the core of all this, is you. Your mind, your body and your soul. Generally, when you're busy and passionately trying to change the world, the mind tends to reign supreme, resulting in our physical, emotional and spiritual health being relegated to the back seat

… and often taking a beating. Taking on the challenge of doing good in the world, with the added pressure of getting paid for it, is the work of warriors. But most actual warriors go through years of training, whereas you or I might just dive in head first, and pretty quickly realize we're out of our depth. On top of that, a lot of the things we care about – social justice and inequality, the climate and ecological emergency, the relentless march of globalization – are massive juggernauts that may take decades to slow or stop.

So how do we prioritize self-care and make sure our efforts aren't making us, or those around us, anxious, depressed, overwhelmed or paralysed with fear? We make self-care top of the list. One of my all-time favourite sayings is, 'You should sit in meditation for 20 minutes a day. Unless you're too busy, in which case you should sit for an hour.' Those Zen monks knew a thing or two.

I remember thinking to myself one day, 'Oh this is what it feels like to be relaxed...'

A burnt-out, stressed-out version of you won't further your cause, so nourish yourself deeply, keep your tanks topped up and let the good times roll.

I speak from experience. Just two years into City to Sea, I burned out. I'd been saying yes to everything, driving things forward, working long hours and not taking care of myself properly. I'd jumped into setting up the organization straight from a full-on day job in TV, too, so my stress levels were already seriously high, although I didn't clock it at the time. In late 2017 things came to a head when the triple whammy of a relationship break-up, a house-move and a TED talk all landed in the same month. I was beyond tired, emotional, anxious and finding it hard to concentrate, and I'd started having digestive problems, which would later be diagnosed as a hiatus hernia, most likely caused by stress. Oops. In my ambition to make City to Sea a success and to make a serious dent in plastic pollution, I'd run myself ragged.

Thanks to the team I had around me at the time I was able to take some time out and spend a couple of weeks recovering my mojo and unpacking boxes in my new home. I knew I didn't want to feel that way again, although it wasn't until the COVID-19 pandemic wiped out my diary of speaking engagements and travel that I got to stop properly, for long enough for my body to remember how it felt not to be stressed. In fact, I don't think I'd stopped for that long for most of my adult life, and, despite the worrying circumstances, the break felt good. I had more sleep, less travel, fewer meetings and more time in the sunshine in my garden. I remember thinking to myself one day, 'Oh, this is what it feels like to be relaxed. I like it. Let's try and keep this feeling close.'

To stay on an even keel, we need to restore and regenerate our insides at the same time as restoring and regenerating the planet. Burnout sucks, but it can be avoided by creating a self-care programme that works for you. Here are my top tips:

Get outside
If you can't get out into nature daily, even just your backyard or local park, make time for it at weekends. A study published in the journal *Environmental Science & Technology* in 2010 found

that just five minutes of exercise (including walking or gardening – you don't have to do 50 star jumps) in a park, backyard garden, nature trail or other green space benefit mental health.[15] And a study from the University of Exeter in 2019 found that a two-hour 'dose' of nature once a week significantly boosts health and well-being, even if you're just sitting on your arse doing nothing.[16] You don't have to get that dose in one hit, either, because the study found that the benefits were the same if you took lots of smaller visits to green spaces.

Get a morning routine
I know these are supposed to be really important, but I've always been shit at them. I am not one of those super-productive-before-8am people, but more of a fanny about, have a cup of coffee, do some meditation or exercise kinda gal. But apparently successful people do morning routines, so you might want to give it a go. For inspiration, check out Hal Elrod's book *Miracle Morning: The Not-So-Obvious Secret Guaranteed to Transform your Life (Before 8am)* (2012). He's got it nailed in six minutes. Then throw in Dr Zach Bush's four-minute workout for good measure (see zachbushmd.com) and get your nitric oxide pumped and dumped, baby!

Make a plan
We talked about project-management tools on page 185, but they can also have a positive effect on your mental health. Knowing what step you need to take next to reach your goal can help stop overwhelm, as you see that it doesn't all need doing right now. And you can write tomorrow's to-do list at the end of the day, so you're not stressing or worrying about

tasks or workload when you should be having some downtime. From digital to-do lists to sexy stationery, having a clear idea of your daily tasks frees up your inner space and gives you a sense of being on top of things, even if you're not.

Protect your most productive time

It's easy to let time run away with you (especially if you think it's a good idea to check your social media channels before your morning meditation or walk) or allow it to be taken up by other people's agendas. So be fiercely protective of your most productive time, and keep that for yourself. If you're a morning person, block out two hours in your diary between 10am and 12pm so that no one can disturb you and you can do your best work. If you're part of a team, suggest a 'meeting-free day' (or morning) each week so that you can all get the big stuff done.

... be fiercely protective of your most productive time, and keep that for yourself.

If you're physically able, make time for daily exercise. Studies and scientists galore tell us that exercise is one of the best ways to de-stress, get happy and sustain your energy levels. Twenty minutes a day is the standard, recommended amount, but even if you can do that only three days a week you're still winning. If you're really not an exercise person, build it into your daily activities: try to run, walk or cycle to work; take the stairs instead of the lift; or get a dog (if you can look after it properly) to make you leave the house. If you can't manage that, seven minutes a day is better than nothing. The seven-minute workout (basically a high-intensity interval training or HIIT workout; there are lots of variations online) has been proven to have huge health benefits, including better cardio health, increased endurance and weight loss. When all else fails, fall back on Dr Zach Bush's four-minute workout (see page 195). If you're living with a physical impairment or condition, try to find a form of daily exercise that works for you and keeps you pepped and pumped, or, if exercise isn't an option, explore breath work to keep your stress levels low (I recommend James Nestor's *Breath: The New Science of a Lost Art*, 2020).

Book in holidays
This is especially important when you're working for yourself, because it can easily fall off the radar. A study in 2019 showed that it takes at least three days to de-stress, but that eight days is the ideal length for a vacation. Another found that even a quick getaway of four nights (staycations encouraged!) can decrease stress and strain for up to 45 days after the return home.[17] If you're in the early days of getting your project off the ground and have little spare cash, don't forget that holidays needn't be expensive. Get creative with house swaps, camping trips and last-minute deals on coach and rail travel.

Social media
Try to develop a mindful, conscious approach to your social media use to protect your time, energy and mental health. It's a fantastic tool for creating community, spreading awareness and educating yourself, but it is designed to get you hooked. Clever algorithms play into our fears and aspirations, so try to

be the one who's in control, instead of letting it control you. A good way to do this is to set boundaries around when you use it. For example, I don't let myself go on social media and check my notifications and messages until I've done my morning meditation, and then I limit it to about half an hour. If you're using it for work, try setting aside time in your working day to engage with your audience and do what you need to do, then leave it alone. Turn off notifications, and for extra clarity and boundaries, use a separate phone for your work stuff.

Get good sleep
This is a bit unfair, isn't it? Some people can just switch off and lie like a log for nine hours, whereas others are wide-eyed, brain buzzing, staring into the night. But check you're doing all you can to give yourself the best chance of a good night's sleep. Get an evening wind-down routine: switch screens off an hour before bed, put your phone on flight mode, switch off the WiFi (the bees will thank you for it, too), drink a good-quality sleepy herbal tea, spritz some lavender on your pillow, write tomorrow's to-do list so that you're not thinking about it overnight (and keep a notepad next to your bed so you can write down anything that's bugging you if you're awake), and keep your sleeping space clear of clutter.

Prioritize your mental, emotional and spiritual well-being
When things get busy, stress and overwhelm can easily creep up on you. This can be avoided with gentle prompts, reminders and tools to keep you nourished and radiating good stuff. One person's food for the soul is another's turn-off, so make time to find the things that are a big 'yes' for you. You might gravitate

to one of the great apps that are designed to support your mental health, such as CALM and Insight Timer. Or you might find your peace on a sweaty dance floor, self-pleasuring in the bedroom, or whipping up a storm in the kitchen. Whatever works for you, schedule it, protect it and do it. Often.

Eat well

Eat organic and eat the rainbow. A healthy diet helps you maintain a healthy body and mind. However, it's easy to let it slip when you're feeling pushed for time and focused on work. A bit of forward planning goes a long way. I get an organic fruit and veg box delivered each week to make sure I've got my dose of local goodness. If you can eat nuts, roast them up with soy or tamari sauce to give you tasty little energy nuggets for snacks. Using a blender or juicer is another great way to help you get your zingy, raw kicks in.

Remember that there are some wonderful, well-trained, caring professionals out there if things start to get on top of you. In fact, I'd recommend having a couple whom you see regularly – for therapy, body work or coaching – *before* things get too much. That's good self-care. So is talking to your friends, colleagues and medical professionals about your feelings. It's OK to be vulnerable, it's OK to feel shitty, and it's very much OK to ask for help.

NEXT STEPS

It's a bold move, changing the world. And it's a rewarding one. So gather your strength, let go of your attachment to outcomes, and get going. They say a journey of a thousand miles begins with one step, so that's all you need to focus on. I hope that by now you've got a plan and plenty of ideas about funding it. You'll have a sense of the people you need to have around you and the ways to communicate, and an understanding of how important it is to measure and evaluate your activities – especially if you want to keep doing them and keep generating an income. With luck, you're bursting with excitement, a sense of possibility, and confidence in your capacity to pull this off, or at least have a blast giving it your best shot.

Doing work that does good in the world has a magical alchemy. It doesn't just change what's going on out there and the people whose lives you're affecting; it changes what's going on inside you. Something inexplicable and intangible, but most definitely noticeable, happens when you're serving the greater good. It's not just the warm, fuzzy feeling of altruism – although that in itself is valuable – it's an actual transformation of your energy. Obviously, you don't need to take my word for it. But if you're curious, or a bit baffled by this idea, read my book *The Everyday Alchemist's Happiness Handbook* (2012). Essentially, when serving others by dedicating yourself to love, harmony and justice – even if that means fighting for it – you're healing yourself and the world. And when you do that, good things come.

Going it alone can be dull, though, so if you've not already aligned yourself with a community working on the same issue, or surrounded yourself with inspirational, positive allies who want to help you succeed, start there. Without shoulders to cry on, arms to link with, hands to hold, or feet and wheels to march and dance with, it's all a bit meaningless. And meaning is what we're after, more than money – all the feels that come with creating and building something that's made a difference, that's changed the world for the better. Yes, we need food on the table, warm beds and freedom from financial worries. But it's the more beautiful world we're creating that ultimately feeds us, and when you're aligned with that, the rest might even take care of itself. There's a better way than the one that got us into this mess, and getting out of it can be way more fun.

Finally, a reminder to be brave and ask for what you need. Ask clearly, ask often and ask without expectation. Your mission is important and your precious time here is limited, so believe in yourself and get out there – go do good and get paid.

And if you want to say hi along the way, or share in your struggles or successes, you can find me on Instagram @nataliefee_.

Shine on!

Natalie x

ENDNOTES

1. See Jack McCullough, 'The Psychopathic CEO', Forbes, 9 December 2019, www.forbes.com/sites/jackmccullough/2019/12/09/the-psychopathic-ceo.

2. George Monbiot, 'Public Luxury for All or Private Luxury for Some: This Is the Choice We Face', *The Guardian*, 31 May 2017, www.theguardian.com/commentisfree/2017/may/31/private-wealth-labour-common-space.

3. 'A Family of Four Needs £40,000 a Year to Make Ends Meet', Heart Lifestyle, 4 July 2018, www.heart.co.uk/lifestyle/parenting/national-family-income-wage-to-live-in-uk.

4. Jami Farkas, 'This Is the Living Wage You Need in All 50 States', GOBankingRates, 5 June 2021, www.gobankingrates.com/money/jobs/living-wage-every-state.

5. 'Money Only Buys Happiness for a Certain Amount', Purdue University, 13 February 2018, www.purdue.edu/newsroom/releases/2018/Q1/money-only-buys-happiness-for-a-certain-amount.html.

6. 'Does Money Buy Happiness? Find Out How Much You Need to Be Happy Around the World', Raisin, 1 July 2020, www.raisin.co.uk/newsroom/articles/does-money-buy-happiness.

7. Average Salary Survey, www.averagesalarysurvey.com/costa-rica.

8. Riichiro Ishida, 'Reducing Anxiety in Stutterers Through the Association Between "Purpose in Life/Ikigai" and Emotions',

Global Journal of Health Science, IV/5 (September 2012), pp. 120–4, www.ncbi.nlm.nih.gov/pmc/articles/PMC4776915.

9. Joseph Folkman, '8 Ways to Ensure your Vision Is Valued', Forbes, 22 April 2014, www.forbes.com/sites/joefolkman/2014/04/22/8-ways-to-ensure-your-vision-is-valued.

10. D. Clark, 'Average Amount Given to Charity per Charitable Giver in the England from 2013/14 to 2020/21', Statista, 16 August 2021, www.statista.com/statistics/292949/average-amount-given-to-charity-per-giver-in-england-uk-y-on-y.

11. See en.wikipedia.org/wiki/Ice_Bucket_Challenge.

12. Tom Sheppard, 'Determining the Right Legal Structure for your Social Enterprise', UnLtd, www.unltd.org.uk/learn/determining-the-right-legal-structure-for-your-social-enterprise.

13. Brandon Busteed and Zac Auter, 'Why Colleges Should Make Internships a Requirement', Gallup blog, 27 November 2017, news.gallup.com/opinion/gallup/222497/why-colleges-internships-requirement.aspx.

14. See disappearingelephants.com/overview.

15. 'In the Green of Health: Just 5 Minutes of "Green" Exercise Optimal for Good Mental Health', ScienceDaily, 21 May 2010, www.sciencedaily.com/releases/2010/05/100502080414.htm.

16. Damian Carrington, 'Two-hour "Dose" of Nature Significantly Boosts Health – Study', *The Guardian*, 13 June 2019, www.theguardian.com/environment/2019/jun/13/two-hour-dose-nature-weekly-boosts-health-study-finds.

17. Cornelia Blank et al., 'Short Vacation Improves Stress-Level and Well-Being in German-Speaking Middle-Managers: A Randomized Controlled Trial', *International Journal of Environmental and Residential Public Health*, XV/1 (January 2018), p. 130, www.ncbi.nlm.nih.gov/pmc/articles/PMC5800229.

ACKNOWLEDGEMENTS

My thanks, first and foremost, go to my team at City to Sea. It goes without saying that this book wouldn't exist without them. Especially Rebecca Burgess, my 'Integrator' for two years, for showing me the power of two (we hadn't even read *Rocket Fuel* back then!), and my SLT, Jo Morley, for her relentless passion and energy; Jane Martin for her capacity to dream big while juggling an insane number of balls; Megan Hewlett for her attention to detail, heavy lifting and all the stuff I'm terrible at; and Hetti Dysch for keeping things wild and witchy. I'm honoured to have you all by my side. To the wider team, thank you for choosing to do good and get paid on board the good ship City to Sea, and for sticking with us through the storms. You're the reason we're still sailing. And to the advisors, board members and trustees, thank you for giving your time and energy to the cause and for your belief, encouragement and expertise – you're all, past and present, hugely appreciated.

To my mentor, Steve Clark, you've been the wind in my sails on so many occasions, and this book wouldn't exist without you either. Thank you for being so utterly amazing. To my Director's Club crew – Hamish, Tom, Matt, Dan, Lorrin and Paula – you're all awesome and I'm incredibly grateful for the fireside chats (real ones, with fire!), after-hours calls and extra support (even illustrations) you've all gifted me. And to my Coralus mentor, MJ Ryan, and the whole Coralus community, a radically generous network of kick-ass business womxn who are a constant reminder of how wonderful human beings really are.

To Nick Hounsfield and Craig Stoddart at the Wave for all the love, guidance, free desks and free lunches when we were just starting out.

To my literary agent, Jane Graham-Maw, for believing in me and my mission and helping me get my story out to a wider audience, and to Zara Larcombe for commissioning it. To the team at Laurence King Publishing, it's been a total pleasure to work with you again, and thank you for co-creating something that will hopefully help make the world a better place. To Holly Cookston-Williams, Lily O'Brien, Sally Beare and Traci Lewis, thank you for your support with research and organizing case studies when I needed you most.

To the changemakers featured in this book – Christian Kroll, Sabia Wade, Kumi Naidoo, Hera Hussain, Traci Lewis, Danny Renton, Valentino Barrioseta, Sarah Corbett and Atif Choudhury – it's been an honour, a delight and a learning experience for me to spend time with each of you and hear your stories. Thank you *so* much for saying yes, sharing your journeys and learnings with me and my readers, and making our world that little bit brighter.

INDEX

LAURENCE KING

First published in Great Britain in 2023
by Laurence King, an imprint of
The Orion Publishing Group Ltd
Carmelite House, 50 Victoria
Embankment, London EC4Y 0DZ

An Hachette UK Company

10 9 8 7 6 5 4 3 2 1

A CIP catalogue record for this book
is available from the British Library.

ISBN 978-0-8578-2919-1

Senior Editor: Katherine Pitt
Design: Hannah Owens

Origination by F1 Colour Ltd, London

Printed in China by C&C Offset Printing Co. Ltd

MIX
Paper | Supporting
responsible forestry
FSC® C104740

www.laurenceking.com
www.orionbooks.co.uk